Distingu Pr

"Living Proverbs"—Vol. 4

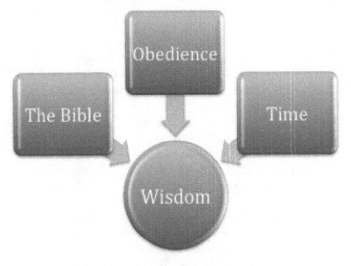

—Over 530 New Wisdom Insights
For Contemporary Times—

Pastor Terrance Levise Turner, MBA

Well Spoken Inc. | *Nashville, TN*

Unless otherwise indicated, all Scripture quotations are taken from the King James Version of the Bible. Unless otherwise indicated all original quotes are those of
Pastor Terrance Levise Turner.

Well Spoken Inc.
P.O. Box 291806 Nashville, TN. 37229
WellSpokenInc@bellsouth.net
www.TerranceTurnerBooks.com

Ordering Information

Quantity sales. Special discounts are available on quantity purchases by corporations, associations, and others. For details, contact the "Special Sales Department" at the address above.

Cover design by Ryan Urz/Susan of LSDdesign/99Designs.com
Book design by Terrance L. Turner

Printed in the United States of America

ISBN   9781733979603   and   9781733979610   paperback
ISBN   9780999323694   and   9781733979627   hardcover

Also by Pastor Terrance Levise Turner, MBA:

Distinguished Wisdom Presents... Living Proverbs–Volume 1

Distinguished Wisdom Presents... Living Proverbs–Volume 2

Distinguished Wisdom Presents... Living Proverbs–Volume 3

Distinguished Wisdom Presents... The Dynamic Victory Confession: Powerful Confessions For A Victorious Life!

The Earth Is Sad, Little Timmy

Distinguished Wisdom Presents... Your Wealth Is In Your Anointing: Discover Keys To Releasing Your Potential.

This book is dedicated to young people of today and in future generations. I desire that they have a solid understanding of God and His principles for life; and thereby have a successful, prosperous, safe, and godly life.

Contents

Acknowledgments... VII

Preface...IX

Introduction XI

"Living Proverbs" –Vol. 4 1

Final Word.. 257

About The Author 259

V

Acknowledgments

I would like to acknowledge the love and support of my wife, Dr. Avis Turner. She is my partner in life, and the gift that God has given me to help accomplish His purposes in life. Her support and encouragement has helped to enable me to reach the potential God has invested in me. She is a *true* wife. We are better together, and together God is enabling us to reach the world.

Again, I would like to give everlasting thanks to my mother, Geraldine Key, for the foundation of truth and example she laid for my brothers and I. She is the reason I know God as my Heavenly Father and the Lord Jesus Christ as my Savior. She continues to be a support and encouragement as I strive to fulfill God's purposes for my life.

I acknowledge the solid example of faith, faithfulness, and morality that I gained from my grandmother, Wilma Starks, and grandfather, Clarence Young. They both were sources of stability in my life. Their examples will continue to live on in all that I do.

I thank God for all the teachers and preachers of wisdom and instruction over my lifetime. Thank God for Rev. Brockway, Bishop Phillip Gardner, missionary Mary Archie, Pastor Charles Cowan, Bishop T.D. Jakes, Joyce Meyer, Dr. Mike Murdock, and many others that has inspired my life. Thank God for inspirational and motivational teachers, such as Les Brown, Brian Tracy, Dr. John Maxwell; as well as great leaders in our society, such as Gen. Colin Powell. Also, I recognize the impact of great educational leaders upon my life, such as the late Dr. James A. Hefner, former president of Tennessee State University. My life has been impacted by great leaders in wisdom, instruction, and by example. My mother laid the foundation, and Jehovah God my Heavenly Father has built upon that foundation the right keystones, starting with my wife, Dr. Avis Turner, for a successful life.

Preface

My mother introduced my brothers and I, to God as our Father by teaching us the principles of the Book of Proverbs in the Bible. She sat down with us in Bible studies and prayer, and taught us the principles of morality, godliness, and wisdom for life that the Book of Proverbs contained. She took us to church and she lived the principles of God's Word before us in our home. My mother's dedication to the Lord Jesus Christ was my example for seeing how to live a life sanctified unto God. Through her example, along with my grandmother, I gained a deep love for God and His principles.

As I grew up and became an adult, I continued to look to God's Word as the source of wisdom for life. The Book of Proverbs became a mainstay of reliable wisdom for my life. The structure of the book and the manner in which the truths were conveyed were easy for me to digest. They are direct, bite-sized, concentrated nuggets of truth. This affected and helped to craft and shape my thinking.

Distinguished Wisdom Presents... Living Proverbs came into being gradually, day by day. I was led by God to begin sharing the wisdom, which I had learned and ascertained from walking with Him, with others that could be enlighten and encouraged by what was offered.

Living Proverbs came into being in real-time from me being led by the Spirit and sharing with others what I believed would minister to their lives. My prayer is that they will minister to you now and in time to come.

Introduction

Historical Aspects of Biblical Proverbs

1 Kings 3:4–14 gives the account of King Solomon becoming king after his father King David died. He, though a full grown man, felt as if he was a child in regards to taking over such an immense responsibility to reign as king, especially after such a notable mark, which his father had made on the kingdom of Israel and history.

Solomon prayed to God for wisdom to rule justly and with good understanding for God's people. The following passage describes the account:

> And the king went to Gibeon to sacrifice there; for that was the great high place: a thousand burnt offerings did Solomon offer upon that altar.
>
> In Gibeon the Lord appeared to Solomon in a dream by night: and God said, Ask what I shall give thee.
>
> And Solomon said, Thou hast shewed unto thy servant David my father great mercy, according

as he walked before thee in truth, and in righteousness, and in uprightness of heart with thee; and thou hast kept for him this great kindness, that thou hast given him a son to sit on his throne, as it is this day.

And now, O Lord my God, thou hast made thy servant king instead of David my father: and I am but a little child: I know not how to go out or come in.

And thy servant is in the midst of thy people which thou hast chosen, a great people, that cannot be numbered nor counted for multitude.

Give therefore thy servant an understanding heart to judge thy people, that I may discern between good and bad: for who is able to judge this thy so great a people?

And the speech pleased the Lord, that Solomon had asked this thing.

And God said unto him, Because thou hast asked this thing, and hast not asked for thyself long life; neither hast asked riches for thyself, nor hast asked the life of thine enemies; but hast asked for thyself understanding to discern judgment;

Behold, I have done according to thy words: lo, I have given thee a wise and an understanding heart; so that there was none like thee before thee, neither after thee shall any arise like unto thee.

And I have also given thee that which thou hast not asked, both riches, and honour: so that there shall not be any among the kings like unto thee all thy days.

And if thou wilt walk in my ways, to keep my statutes and my commandments, as thy father David did walk, then I will lengthen thy days.

–1 Kings 3:4–14

So, we see that God gave King Solomon wisdom to reign over His people; unlike any other king. The wisdom, which Solomon obtained, was the key to great riches, honor, and renown.

Solomon was a teacher. He was a preacher as well. He taught his sons and others his wisdom using proverbs, parables, and wise sayings. He felt that this was the best way to help those that heard his wisdom to gain the concepts, which he was attempting to convey to their understanding.

In Ecclesiastes 1:1 King Solomon calls himself the Preacher. This is what it says:

XIII

The words of the Preacher, the son of David, king in Jerusalem.

–Ecclesiastes 1:1

The Book of Proverbs also gives us the biblical purpose of using proverbs, parables, and wise sayings to teach. Proverbs 1:1–7 defines the purpose of the Book of Proverbs, as well as the purpose of this book **Living Proverbs.** This is what it says:

The proverbs of Solomon the son of David, king of Israel;

To **know** wisdom and instruction; to **perceive** the words of understanding;

To **receive** the instruction of wisdom, justice, and judgment, and equity;

To give **subtilty** to the simple, to the young man knowledge and discretion.

A wise man will hear, and will increase learning; and a man of understanding shall attain unto wise counsels:

To **understand** a proverb, and the **interpretation**; the words of the wise, and their dark sayings.

The fear of the Lord is the beginning of knowledge: but fools despise wisdom and instruction.

–Proverbs 1:1–7

Notice, that I bolded a few key words in this passage of scripture, which I would like to point out to you. They clearly explain the purpose of the biblical Book of Proverbs, as well as this book **Living Proverbs.**

The first word that I would like to point out is the word **know.**

The Strongs Exhaustive Concordance of The Bible defines this word like this:

> **3045– yada**
>
> 1. to know or ascertain by seeing
>
> 2. observation, recognition, instruction
>
> 3. acknowledge, acquainted with
>
> 4. to know assuredly
>
> 5. to be aware
>
> 6. to know for a certainty
>
> 7. to cause to discern
>
> 8. to discover

Therefore, based on these definitions, we see that the initial purpose of biblical proverbs is so that the reader may know and ascertain God's wisdom by clearly seeing it. It is to allow the person to observe the deeper meaning of a subject in a condensed way. It is to teach the person how to recognize wisdom when it is being spoken, and to take heed to instruction when it is being given.

The speaking of proverbs is a way of conveying meaning that has been tested and tried as true in a condensed manner that helps them gain the certainty of those truths.

They are given so that people can discern truth when it is being presented, without having to have a full explanation. They will not have to have a full explanation in order to discern the meaning being conveyed.

Proverbs are a condensed conveying of deeper meaning.

The next word, which King Solomon uses to define the purpose of biblical proverbs is **perceive.** This is how the concordance defines it:

> **995–biyn**
>
> 1. To separate mentally or to distinguish
>
> 2. understand
>
> 3. discern
>
> 4. be cunning
>
> 5. diligently
>
> 6. direct

7. to have intelligence

8. deal wisely

Notice, the words used to define perceive are words that deal with the mind. One of the purposes of proverbs of all kinds is for the reader to become more keen in their thinking, and thus, more capable to be successful in life.

The goal is that the person that heeds proverbs will learn to perceive and understand God's ways of doing and being right in life. It is that they will learn to discern right and wrong, as well as timing and manner of doing the right thing.

Through studying proverbs a young person, as well as those more experienced in life, will become more cunning or skillful in navigating decisions, people skills, etc. Various proverbs are given to encourage the reader to become more diligent in life matters; and thus more successful and prosperous.

Short wise sayings, parables, and proverbs can provide swift guidance to a persons decision making. They will direct a persons steps in the midst of a decision making process.

Through heeding various godly proverbs, a person will gain quick intelligence for good judgment. The person that gives themselves to proverbs as a companion to their life will learn to deal wisely in lifes diverse situations.

As a person gives themselves to the study of proverbs, they will learn to **receive** wisdom when it is being presented. They will gain more **subtlety** in life. They will become more discreet and refined in behavior and decision–making and manner; thus, making them better able to smoothly navigate the potentially rough matters of human relationships.

Ultimately, the biblical Book of Proverbs, as well as this book **Living Proverbs** is written so that the person who heeds them may gain a greater **understanding** of God's principles for successful living. Also, that they will be able to **interpret** God's wisdom as it is presented to them, whether through reading the Bible or in the lessons of life.

This is the purpose of this book **Living Proverbs.** My goal in writing this book is to convey the understanding of the Word of God and His principles in a way that it is easy for anyone to understand. My goal is to bring God's Word alive to your understanding.

Insights On Wisdom

What is wisdom? Why is it important? How is it obtained? How is it used?

Wisdom is not knowledge. Wisdom is the discerned, proper application of knowledge, which comes from experience. In this book I utilize several key conceptual scriptures more than once. However, with each usage I bring out a unique perspective or point of view. The wisdom of God's Word is multifaceted. There are layers of truth to be discovered. The name of the book series is ***Distinguished Wisdom Presents . . . "Living Proverbs."*** Each *wisdom nugget* reveals a treasure of truth that has been extracted and refined by understanding. The deeper meaning is conveyed by a few unique and memorable words. The Book of Proverbs in the Bible encourages us to not only get knowledge of the wisdom of God, but to get "understanding".

> Get wisdom, get understanding: forget it not; neither decline from the words of my mouth. Forsake her not, and she shall preserve thee: love her, and she shall keep thee. Wisdom is the principle thing; therefore, get wisdom; and with all thy getting get understanding.
>
> – Proverbs 4: 5–7

Romans 10:17 says, "Faith comes by hearing, and hearing by the Word of God." As you continue to abide in the principles of God's Word, you gain deeper understanding. The Word becomes more usable to you. God wants us to be skillful in the use of His Word for our daily living.

The following scriptures further emphasize the vital importance of wisdom:

> The fear of the Lord is the beginning of knowledge: but fools despise wisdom and instruction.
>
> – Proverbs 1:7

> Also, that the soul be without knowledge, it is not good; and he that hasteth with the feet sinneth.
>
> – Proverbs 19:2

He that getteth wisdom loveth his own soul: he
that keepeth understanding shall find good.

– Proverbs 19:8

Based on these scriptures, we can see that God's wisdom is
vital for successful living. **Distinguished Wisdom Presents...**
Living Proverbs –Vol. 4, helps to further your understanding
and application of God's wisdom for life.

Habakkuk 2:4b says, " . . . *the just shall live by his faith."* In
other words, the only way the faith and wisdom of the Word
of God will work for you is by actually living by what you
learn. As God's Word is lived out in your daily life, it becomes
wisdom gained by experience. You will know with certainty
the reliability of Gods Word. You can then pass that wisdom
on to your family, friends, and those you come in contact with
in your daily life.

Wisdom is for success in daily living. These **Living Proverbs**
were derived from addressing the challenges of my life and
the lives of others. They are original, relevant, Christian
wisdom quotes that will help you on your journey. I have
dealt with many of the same challenges that you have, and I
know God's Word will work for you.

The Purpose of *Living Proverbs.*

The purpose of *Living Proverbs* is derived from the purpose of
my company Well Spoken Incorporated in Nashville,
Tennessee. In 2005, God inspired me to start a company with
the purpose of communicating the spoken word in a clear,

distinct manner that easily conveyed understanding to the listener. The primary product at the start was audio books. The products have since expanded into print, speaking, and other forms of media.

The foundational scripture that inspired the company is Nehemiah 8:7–8. It says,

> Also Jeshua, and Bani, and Sherebiah, Jamin, Akkub, Shabbethai, Hodijah, Maaseiah, Kelita, Azariah, Jozabad, Hanan, Pelaiah, and the Levites, caused the people to understand the law: and the people stood in their place. So they read in the book in the law of God distinctly, and gave the sense, and caused them to understand the reading.

> — Nehemiah 8:7–8

The Levites helped the people to understand the law of God, and the people became secure in their place in the land. They became stable as a result of gaining understanding. The Levites read in the book of the law of God *distinctly*, and gave the *sense* or meaning or policy or prosperity of the scripture. They helped the people to understand what was read. The Levites carried out a specific function to help the people become prosperous through understanding the Word of God that was spoken by the priests.

The scripture says, "So they read in the book of the law of God *distinctly*..." God gave me the brand ***Distinguished Wisdom Presents*** ... from this particular scripture. The

Levites helped the people to *distinguish* what the Word of God was saying or what it really meant. The Webster's dictionary defines *distinguish* as "*to recognize plainly by any of the senses.*" The root meaning is *to prick or pierce apart.* The word *distinct* is defined as "*clearly marked off; plain; well defined; unmistakable.*" God used the Levites to clearly define His Word for the people so that the meaning would be unmistakable. God wanted them to understand His true purpose for giving His laws, which is for our good.

When God gave me the brand and assignment for **Distinguished Wisdom Presents . . .** He indicated to me that he had anointed me to share wisdom in a *distinct* manner. Through my study of the book of Proverbs from childhood, I developed a love for wisdom and the Word of God. My education in communications helped to prepare me to speak God's Word. God gave me the name of the company Well Spoken Incorporated as a way of ministering His Word in a clear, specialized manner for those who needed to understand.

I began to share *Living Proverbs* as wisdom nuggets to friends and followers on social media as a means of spreading God's Word to encourage, inspire, and inform. The platform of social media has allowed an expanded reach of God's Word into the world for both believers as well as secular society. God has a need for those who are willing to share His Word with the world. 2 Chronicles 15:3 indicates God's need for a *willing vessel* to share His Word. This is what it says,

Now for a long season Israel hath been without the true God, and without a teaching priest, and without law.

—2 Chronicles 15:3

God needs "*teaching priests*" who will teach His Word and bring understanding of His laws to society. This is my purpose, to fulfill God's *Great Commission* of spreading His Word and ways to the hearts of His people.

Please enjoy this book as a continual companion of counsel and guidance. All of the **Living Proverbs** are clearly supported by scriptural references. You will be able to have a relevant Bible study with every one of them. Your understanding of God's Word will increase as each layer of meaning is revealed from the scriptures used in this book. Meditate on them. Use it as a reference book. With every page you will find a *nugget* of wisdom that will enrich your daily life.

Now delve into the wisdom of God in **Distinguished Wisdom Presents . . . Living Proverbs–Vol. 4.** *May your life be enriched by the words of wisdom!*

—Pastor Terrance Levise Turner, MBA

"Living Proverbs" –Vol. 4

1601. In once–in–a–lifetime opportunities, you have to use your "*mind–biscuit*" to *sop–up* all of the gravy off of the plate. Tomorrow is not promised. If you are in school, college, or a special training opportunity, be sure to make the most of it. Make it work for you *today*!

Boast not thyself of to morrow; for thou knowest not what a day may bring forth.

–Proverbs 27:1

1602. Handle your space.

Every place that the sole of your foot shall tread upon, that have I given unto you, as I said unto Moses.

– Joshua 1:3

1603. If you can see farther than where you came from, you can go farther, and be more than where you came from.

And they said, Go to, let us build us a city and a tower, whose top may reach unto heaven; and let us make us a name, lest we be scattered abroad upon the face of the whole earth. And the Lord came down to see the city and the tower, which the children of men builded. And the Lord said, Behold, the people is one, and they have all one language; and this they begin to do: and now nothing will be restrained from them, which they have imagined to do.

– Genesis 11:4–6

1604. Harvest season always comes. It may not come as fast as you want it to come, but the more that you truly want it to come, the faster it will come, because you will do what's necessary to *make* it come.

Whatsoever thy hand findeth to do, do it with thy might; for there is no work, nor device, nor knowledge, nor wisdom, in the grave, whither thou goest. I returned, and saw under the sun, that the race is not to the swift, nor the battle to the strong, neither yet bread to the wise, nor yet riches to men of understanding, nor yet favour to men of skill; but time and chance happeneth to them all.

– Ecclesiastes 9:10–11

1605. Keep on serving God, and stay on the *blessing* side of the Word.

I call heaven and earth to record this day against you, that I have set before you life and death, blessing and cursing: therefore choose life, that both thou and thy seed may live.

– Deuteronomy 30:19

1606. If you honor Jesus, and His principles, you will do well. It's not just about loving Jesus. Rather, to be successful, you have to obey the principles of His Word. Jesus will comfort you in your trials. He will give you joy for living. However, you give Him and the Heavenly Father joy by prospering through obeying His principles.

Jesus answered and said unto him, If a man love me, he will keep my words: and my Father will love him, and we will come unto him, and make our abode with him. He that loveth me not keepeth not my sayings: and the word which ye hear is not mine, but the Fathers which sent me.

— John 14:23–24

1607. Be influenced by your neck, but lead with your head.

Wives, submit yourselves unto your own husbands, as unto the Lord. For the husband is the head of the wife, even as Christ is the head of the church: and he is the saviour of the body. Therefore as the church is subject unto Christ, so let the wives be to their own husbands in every thing. Husbands, love your wives, even as Christ also loved the church, and gave himself for it; That he might sanctify and cleanse it with the washing of water by the word, That he might present it to himself a glorious church, not having spot, or wrinkle, or any such thing; but that it should be holy and without blemish. So ought men to love their wives as their own bodies. He that loveth his wife loveth himself. For no man ever yet hated his own flesh; but nourisheth and cherisheth it, even as the Lord the church: For we are members of his body, of his flesh, and of his bones. For this cause shall a man leave his father and mother, and shall be joined unto his wife, and they two shall be one flesh. This is a great mystery: but I speak concerning Christ and the church. Nevertheless let every one of you in particular so love his wife even as himself; and the wife see that she reverence her husband.

– Ephesians 5:22–33

1608. To make your money independent of being dependent is better.

And that ye study to be quiet, and to do your own business, and to work with your own hands, as we commanded you; that ye may walk honestly toward them that are without, and that ye may have lack of nothing.

–1 Thessalonians 4:11–12

1609. When your blessing comes, it's a matter of fulfillment of a promise, and not a matter of a miracle. It may feel like a miracle, because it was a long–time coming, and you're so happy when it comes. However, the promises are guaranteed to come to pass, simply because we obeyed God's principles. God cannot lie. He's guaranteed what He said. We must only obey what He said.

God is not a man, that he should lie; neither the son of man, that he should repent: hath he said, and shall he not do it? or hath he spoken, and shall he not make it good?

–1 Thessalonians 4:11–12

When the Lord turned again the captivity of Zion, we were
like them that dream. Then was our mouth filled with
laughter, and our tongue with singing: then said they among
the heathen, The Lord hath done great things for them.
The Lord hath done great things for us; whereof we are glad.
Turn again our captivity, O Lord, as the streams in the south.
They that sow in tears shall reap in joy. He that goeth forth
and weepeth, bearing precious seed, shall doubtless come
again with rejoicing, bringing his sheaves with him.

– Psalm 126

1610. God is not new at causing people to succeed. What
He has done for others, He will do for you. All you have to do
is obey His principles of faith, wisdom, diligence, and
perseverance.

That ye be not slothful, but followers of them who through
faith and patience inherit the promises.

– Hebrews 6:12

1611. Whatever may be your sorrow, pain, failure, or
disappointment, know that God is your source of redemption,
joy, and lifelong victory. God is for you; God is with you; and
God is in you. Lay down your pain for the joy of the Lord.

The Spirit of the Lord God is upon me; because the Lord hath
anointed me to preach good tidings unto the meek; he hath
sent me to bind up the brokenhearted, to proclaim liberty to
the captives, and the opening of the prison to them that are

bound; To proclaim the acceptable year of the Lord, and the day of vengeance of our God; to comfort all that mourn; To appoint unto them that mourn in Zion, to give unto them beauty for ashes, the oil of joy for mourning, the garment of praise for the spirit of heaviness; that they might be called trees of righteousness, the planting of the Lord, that he might be glorified.

– Isaiah 61:1–3

1612. The full manifestation of favor takes time. However, favor is for a lifetime.

For His anger is but for a moment, but His favor is for a lifetime *or* in His favor is life. Weeping may endure for a night, but joy comes in the morning.

– Psalm 30:5

Amplified Bible, Classic Edition (AMPC)

1613. If God be for you, who can be against you? If God be for you, who else really matters? If God be for you, He can subdue your adversaries.

He suffered no man to do them wrong: yea, he reproved kings for their sakes; Saying, Touch not mine anointed, and do my prophets no harm.

– Psalm 105:14–15

1614. *Be* who you are, and people will see who you are, and you won't have to *say* who you are. You don't have to brag. Let your *works* speak louder than your words.

Even so faith, if it hath not works, is dead, being alone. Yea, a man may say, Thou hast faith, and I have works: shew me thy faith without thy works, and I will shew thee my faith by my works.

– James 2:17–18

1615. You may be frustrated in seeking to find truth, but, don't worry, the truth will *find you.*

Jesus saith unto him, I am the way, the truth, and the life: no man cometh unto the Father, but by me.

– John 14:6

1616. In the Body of Christ, there's often the fear of *self–exaltation* amongst believers. However, I think God has less concern about our self–exaltation as He does for our lack of *self–actualization*. If we will commit to developing ourselves to be what God called us to be, He can train us concerning the rest, through His hand of faithful loving-kindness.

For the earnest expectation of the creature waiteth for the manifestation of the sons of God.

– Romans 8:19

1617. In relationships, sometimes it's not your words that are needed. It's your listening ear. Sometimes just through your time and understanding, people can *untangle themselves.*

Ointment and perfume rejoice the heart: so doth the sweetness of a man's friend by hearty counsel.

– Proverbs 27:9

1618. Success is not a random miracle. Success is a sure process. If you follow success principles, which are available to all, you will succeed. Success is the *norm,* and not the exception. If we follow the sure patterns that have been successfully traversed, recorded, and shared, we will succeed faster. Get wisdom. It's the principal thing for success.

He that walketh with wise men shall be wise: but a companion of fools shall be destroyed.

– Proverbs 13:20

1619. Allow the light of God to fully shine through you this week. Show your difference. Show your love. Show your brilliance. Shine for Jesus. You are the light of the world!

Ye are the salt of the earth: but if the salt have lost his savour, wherewith shall it be salted? it is thenceforth good for nothing, but to be cast out, and to be trodden under foot of men. Ye are the light of the world. A city that is set on an hill cannot be hid. Neither do men light a candle, and put it under a bushel, but on a candlestick; and it giveth light unto all that are in the house. Let your light so shine before men, that they may see your good works, and glorify your Father which is in heaven.

– Matthew 5:13–16

1620. You may have a lot of things to be concerned about, but pray. Jesus is in control. So, you have nothing to worry about.

Rejoice in the Lord alway: and again I say, Rejoice. Let your moderation be known unto all men. The Lord is at hand. Be careful for nothing; but in every thing by prayer and supplication with thanksgiving let your requests be made known unto God. And the peace of God, which passeth all understanding, shall keep your hearts and minds through Christ Jesus. Finally, brethren, whatsoever things are true, whatsoever things are honest, whatsoever things are just, whatsoever things are pure, whatsoever things are lovely, whatsoever things are of good report; if there be any virtue, and if there be any praise, think on these things. Those things, which ye have both learned, and received, and heard, and seen in me, do: and the God of peace shall be with you.

– Philippians 4:4–9

1621. Often, the greatest friendship is *correction*.

Open rebuke is better than secret love. Faithful are the wounds of a friend; but the kisses of an enemy are deceitful.

– Proverbs 27:5–6

1622. Truly great people are *gracious* people.

That thou mayest walk in the way of good men, and keep the paths of the righteous.

– Proverbs 2:20

1623. There's rarely any drawback to being early. But, there's typically always a negative stigma to being late. Particularly, when you're cooperating with busy, diligent people. There's no perfection. Yet, everyone involved should be striving for the same standard of performance.

Say not ye, There are yet four months, and then cometh harvest? behold, I say unto you, Lift up your eyes, and look on the fields; for they are white already to harvest.

– John 4:35

1624. Some days *you* make happen. Some days make *themselves* happen. When you're led by the Holy Spirit your spirit can lead you faster than your mind can conceive. Even when you can't control all of the details or circumstances, the important thing is that you made progress.

For as many as are led by the Spirit of God, they are the sons of God.

– Romans 8:14

1625. You don't need a sign. You need an *assignment*.

Where there is no vision, the people perish: but he that keepeth the law, happy is he.

– Proverbs 29:18

1626. Little people, with little opinions, make little difference. Keep your eyes on the prize. God knows your heart. He knows what you are accomplishing. "Now, faith is the substance of things hoped for, the evidence of things not seen". Just continue to take steps, and let your *results* speak for themselves.

Even so faith, if it hath not works, is dead, being alone. Yea, a man may say, Thou hast faith, and I have works: shew me thy faith without thy works, and I will shew thee my faith by my works.

– James 2:17–18

1627. The first responsibility of a husband and father is to discern and do what *needs* to be done for his wife and family, such as, to provide protection and short–term and long–term provision. Secondarily, he can focus on fulfilling *wants*. He must also have the insight to discern when a *want* rises to the importance of a *need*, and then respond appropriately.

And the Lord visited Sarah as he had said, and the Lord did unto Sarah as he had spoken. For Sarah conceived, and bare Abraham a son in his old age, at the set time of which God had

11

spoken to him. And Abraham called the name of his son that was born unto him, whom Sarah bare to him, Isaac. And Abraham circumcised his son Isaac being eight days old, as God had commanded him. And Abraham was an hundred years old, when his son Isaac was born unto him. And Sarah said, God hath made me to laugh, so that all that hear will laugh with me. And she said, Who would have said unto Abraham, that Sarah should have given children suck? for I have born him a son in his old age. And the child grew, and was weaned: and Abraham made a great feast the same day that Isaac was weaned. And Sarah saw the son of Hagar the Egyptian, which she had born unto Abraham, mocking. Wherefore she said unto Abraham, Cast out this bondwoman and her son: for the son of this bondwoman shall not be heir with my son, even with Isaac. And the thing was very grievous in Abraham's sight because of his son. And God said unto Abraham, Let it not be grievous in thy sight because of the lad, and because of thy bondwoman; in all that Sarah hath said unto thee, hearken unto her voice; for in Isaac shall thy seed be called. And also of the son of the bondwoman will I make a nation, because he is thy seed. And Abraham rose up early in the morning, and took bread, and a bottle of water, and gave it unto Hagar, putting it on her shoulder, and the child, and sent her away: and she departed, and wandered in the wilderness of Beersheba.

– Genesis 21:1–14

1628. Why spend all of your time, energy, and years fighting to be a slave? When you can use that same time, energy, and years to fight to be *free*. Start that business. Study, partner, work, *borrow* if you have to, but by all means necessary, you can succeed, just like any of the companies you see out there that are succeeding. You are intelligent and capable to do what they've done and more. Extraordinary businesses are started and run by ordinary people. *You too have what it takes!*

And that ye study to be quiet, and to do your own business, and to work with your own hands, as we commanded you; that ye may walk honestly toward them that are without, and that ye may have lack of nothing.

−1 Thessalonians 4:11–12

1629. Don't focus so much on waiting on your blessing to come toward you. Rather, focus on doing what's required so that you are moving toward your blessing. Then, and only then, is your blessing *guaranteed!*

A man shall be satisfied with good by the fruit of his mouth: and the recompence of a man's hands shall be rendered unto him.

– Proverbs 12:14

1630. The evident sign of genius is *productivity.*

And God gave Solomon wisdom and understanding exceeding much, and largeness of heart, even as the sand that is on the sea shore.

−1 Kings 4:29

And the king made silver and gold at Jerusalem as plenteous as stones, and cedar trees made he as the sycomore trees that are in the vale for abundance.

–2 Chronicles 1:15

1631. Success is a good *investment*. Once you get started, success is cumulative like *compound interest*.

Give instruction to a wise man, and he will be yet wiser: teach a just man, and he will increase in learning.

– Proverbs 9:9

1632. No matter what you're facing today, know that the Lord is working on your behalf! He loves you!

And we know that all things work together for good to them that love God, to them who are the called according to his purpose. For whom he did foreknow, he also did predestinate to be conformed to the image of his Son, that he might be the firstborn among many brethren.

– Romans 8:28–29

1633. Praying without ceasing doesn't take a longtime. It just takes *oftentimes*.

Rejoice evermore. Pray without ceasing. In every thing give thanks: for this is the will of God in Christ Jesus concerning you.

–1 Thessalonians 5:16–18

1634. Manipulators are often at a loss when a person ceases to allow him or herself to be manipulated by them. They no longer know what to do to get what they want. However, the simple solution is to present your advantages, and then, sincerely ask for what you want, and give the other person an opportunity to choose *"yes" or "no"*.

Not for that we have dominion over your faith, but are helpers of your joy: for by faith ye stand.

–2 Corinthians 1:24

1635. You're young enough for your dreams. You're strong enough for your dreams. You know enough to obtain your dreams. And you're well able to *possess your land*!

And they told him, and said, We came unto the land whither thou sentest us, and surely it floweth with milk and honey; and this is the fruit of it. Nevertheless the people be strong that dwell in the land, and the cities are walled, and very great: and moreover we saw the children of Anak there. The Amalekites dwell in the land of the south: and the Hittites, and the Jebusites, and the Amorites, dwell in the mountains: and the Canaanites dwell by the sea, and by the coast of Jordan. And Caleb stilled the people before Moses, and said, Let us go up at once, and possess it; for we are well able to overcome it.

– Numbers 13:27–30

1636. Anytime is a good time to take a praise break unto God for all of His goodness, mercy, and loving–kindness to you and your family! Praise Him! It will make you feel better! He deserves it. It's all about Him after all!

It is a good thing to give thanks unto the Lord, and to sing praises unto thy name, O Most High: To shew forth thy lovingkindness in the morning, and thy faithfulness every night.

– Psalm 92:1–2

1637. No matter how you're helped by another person, always be aware of the tendency of human beings to want to control something. Whether it's a dog, a cat, a bird, or another human being, people always try to control someone else. So, always know your value, and demand mutual respect in relationships.

The rich and poor meet together: the Lord is the maker of them all.

– Proverbs 22:2

1638. Control yourself, and you won't be controlled by anyone else.

Watch and pray, that ye enter not into temptation: the spirit indeed is willing, but the flesh is weak.

– Matthew 26:41

1639. Logic lacking love leads to licensing the legalization of lawless deeds, such as abortion, euthanasia, legalizing illegal drugs, genocide, slavery, etc. Logic lacking love leads to licensing the legalization of lawless deeds.

And because iniquity shall abound, the love of many shall wax cold.

– Matthew 24:12

This know also, that in the last days perilous times shall come. For men shall be lovers of their own selves, covetous, boasters, proud, blasphemers, disobedient to parents, unthankful, unholy, Without natural affection, trucebreakers, false accusers, incontinent, fierce, despisers of those that are good, Traitors, heady, highminded, lovers of pleasures more than lovers of God; Having a form of godliness, but denying the power thereof: from such turn away.

–2 Timothy 3:1–5

1640. Give a person food while he or she is hungry. Help a person when he or she is in need.

The full soul loatheth an honeycomb; but to the hungry soul every bitter thing is sweet.

– Proverbs 27:7

1641. It's good to get outside consultation and help. However, always keep the main thing, the main thing, and keep your *core* strong. For this is from where everything emanates. *You* are your source of wealth. Your wealth is released through your fellowship with Christ.

Abide in me, and I in you. As the branch cannot bear fruit of itself, except it abide in the vine; no more can ye, except ye abide in me. I am the vine, ye are the branches: He that abideth in me, and I in him, the same bringeth forth much fruit: for without me ye can do nothing.

– John 15:4–5

1642. The wisdom nature of God is rarely seen in human interactions. Even amongst Christians. However, it is the only true nature of God.

Who is a wise man and endued with knowledge among you? let him shew out of a good conversation his works with meekness of wisdom. But if ye have bitter envying and strife in your hearts, glory not, and lie not against the truth. This wisdom descendeth not from above, but is earthly, sensual, devilish. For where envying and strife is, there is confusion and every evil work. But the wisdom that is from above is first pure, then peaceable, gentle, and easy to be intreated, full of mercy and good fruits, without partiality, and without hypocrisy. And the fruit of righteousness is sown in peace of them that make peace.

– James 3:13–18

1643. In business and relationships, increased contacts equal increased results.

He that walketh with wise men shall be wise: but a companion of fools shall be destroyed.

– Proverbs 13:20

1644. The *old horse* knows the path.

That thou mayest walk in the way of good men, and keep the paths of the righteous.

– Proverbs 2:20

He that walketh with wise men shall be wise: but a companion of fools shall be destroyed

– Proverbs 13:20

1645. What do you get a woman for her birthday when she seems to carry everything around in her purse? Answer: A brand new kitchen sink. Then, she can truly carry everything around, *including* the kitchen sink!

Wherefore seeing we also are compassed about with so great a cloud of witnesses, let us lay aside every weight, and the sin which doth so easily beset us, and let us run with patience the race that is set before us, Looking unto Jesus the author and finisher of our faith; who for the joy that was set before him endured the cross, despising the shame, and is set down at the right hand of the throne of God. For consider him that endured such contradiction of sinners against himself, lest ye be wearied and faint in your minds. Ye have not yet resisted unto blood, striving against sin.

– Hebrews 12:1–4

1646. Keep sowing good seed, because during harvest time, only the seed you've actually sown will come up!

In the morning sow thy seed, and in the evening withhold not thine hand: for thou knowest not whether shall prosper, either this or that, or whether they both shall be alike good.

– Ecclesiastes 11:6

1647. The greatest lesson that you can learn in life is the ability to think for yourself.

But let every man prove his own work, and then shall he have rejoicing in himself alone, and not in another.

– Galatians 6:4

1648. Cynics and critics help you to self–examine what you have to offer. If you really have something of value, you can actually find a better way of presenting it, so that even your cynics and critics can accept it as just being true and good, whether they appreciate the *messenger* or not.

The prophet that hath a dream, let him tell a dream; and he that hath my word, let him speak my word faithfully. What is the chaff to the wheat? saith the Lord. Is not my word like as a fire? saith the Lord; and like a hammer that breaketh the rock in pieces?

— Jeremiah 23:28–29

1649. In the game of life, if you want to play, you had better pray!

And he spake a parable unto them *to this end*, that men ought always to pray, and not to faint.

— Luke 18:1

1650. The difference between undergrad and an MBA program is "it's not personal, it's just business."

For when for the time ye ought to be teachers, ye have need that one teach you again which be the first principles of the oracles of God; and are become such as have need of milk, and not of strong meat. For every one that useth milk is unskilful in the word of righteousness: for he is a babe. But strong meat belongeth to them that are of full age, even those who by reason of use have their senses exercised to discern both good and evil.

— Hebrews 5:12–14

1651. You are the salt of the earth. You are the preservative for the earth, to keep it fresh and alive, and to keep it from being corrupted. If you do not show forth the virtues of God, you will allow the earth to go to corruption. So show forth the virtues of God, which is the fruit of the Spirit (love, joy, peace, longsuffering, gentleness, goodness, faith, meekness, and temperance), and you will keep life fresh and alive!

Ye are the salt of the earth: but if the salt have lost his savour, wherewith shall it be salted? it is thenceforth good for nothing, but to be cast out, and to be trodden under foot of men. Ye are the light of the world. A city that is set on an hill cannot be hid. Neither do men light a candle, and put it under a bushel, but on a candlestick; and it giveth light unto all that are in the house. Let your light so shine before men, that they may see your good works, and glorify your Father, which is in heaven.

– Matthew 5:13–16

1652. There's no better time to solve a problem than when it is a problem, so that it won't continue to be a problem.

The beginning of strife is as when one letteth out water: therefore leave off contention, before it be meddled with.

– Proverbs 17:14

1653. You don't have to be hateful to be truthful.

But speaking the truth in love, may grow up into him in all things, which is the head, *even* Christ.

– Ephesians 4:15

1654. If you want to please God, just start moving in the direction. He knows your heart and He's not looking for perfection. Start taking steps, step by step, and God will get you there. He's always there to help. He always truly cares.

Humble yourselves therefore under the mighty hand of God, that he may exalt you in due time: Casting all your care upon him; for he careth for you. Be sober, be vigilant; because your adversary the devil, as a roaring lion, walketh about, seeking whom he may devour: Whom resist stedfast in the faith, knowing that the same afflictions are accomplished in your brethren that are in the world.

–1 Peter 5:6–9

1655. If you respect money, money will respect you. If you disrespect money, money will leave you. Respecting money means to be watchful over it. Tend to it, take care of it, and it will stay with you. If you disrespect it, it will fly away from you like an eagle toward the heavens!

Wilt thou set thine eyes upon that which is not? for riches certainly make themselves wings; they fly away as an eagle toward heaven.

– Proverbs 23:5

1656. Concerning life, you better *kick* as high as you can, while you still can kick, because soon someone else will be taking your shoes off!

Whatsoever thy hand findeth to do, do it with thy might; for there is no work, nor device, nor knowledge, nor wisdom, in the grave, whither thou goest. I returned, and saw under the sun, that the race is not to the swift, nor the battle to the strong, neither yet bread to the wise, nor yet riches to men of understanding, nor yet favour to men of skill; but time and chance happeneth to them all.

– Ecclesiastes 9:10–11

1657. Don't live your life only looking for miracles. Rather, live your life based on God's existing success principles. Then, you can believe God for His miracle working power to work on your behalf, based on your submission to existing principles.

But rather seek ye the kingdom of God; and all these things shall be added unto you. Fear not, little flock; for it is your Fathers good pleasure to give you the kingdom. Sell that ye have, and give alms; provide yourselves bags which wax not old, a treasure in the heavens that faileth not, where no thief approacheth, neither moth corrupteth. For where your treasure is, there will your heart be also.

– Luke 12:31–34

1658. May God surround you with His favor and anointing like *seven layers of fat* protecting the core of your being.

For thou, Lord, wilt bless the righteous; with favour wilt thou compass him as with a shield.

– Psalm 5:12

1659. If you show a little *hunger*, wisdom will come searching for you. Wisdom is for the wise: those wise enough to know that they need it.

Yea, if thou criest after knowledge, and liftest up thy voice for understanding; If thou seekest her as silver, and searchest for her as for hid treasures; Then shalt thou understand the fear of the Lord, and find the knowledge of God. For the Lord giveth wisdom: out of his mouth cometh knowledge and understanding. He layeth up sound wisdom for the righteous: he is a buckler to them that walk uprightly. He keepeth the paths of judgment, and preserveth the way of his saints. Then shalt thou understand righteousness, and judgment, and equity; yea, every good path. When wisdom entereth into thine heart, and knowledge is pleasant unto thy soul; Discretion shall preserve thee, understanding shall keep thee: To deliver thee from the way of the evil man, from the man that speaketh froward things.

– Proverbs 2:3–12

1660. Identity is not based on circumstances. Identity is based on *DNA*–(Determining–New–Acknowledgments). If you take time to acknowledge who you really are, in spite of circumstances, your circumstances will change, because you will become a new creature. Identity is based on DNA–(Determining–New–Acknowledgments).

That the communication of thy faith may become effectual by the acknowledging of every good thing which is in you in Christ Jesus.

– Philemon 6:1

1661. If you will outlast the devil, the devil will lose, because you've already won. It is the *"good fight of faith"*, because you have already won. Yet, you must resist the devil, and he will flee from you.

Finally, my brethren, be strong in the Lord, and in the power of his might. Put on the whole armour of God, that ye may be able to stand against the wiles of the devil. For we wrestle not against flesh and blood, but against principalities, against powers, against the rulers of the darkness of this world, against spiritual wickedness in high places. Wherefore take unto you the whole armour of God, that ye may be able to withstand in the evil day, and having done all, to stand. Stand therefore, having your loins girt about with truth, and having on the breastplate of righteousness; And your feet shod with the preparation of the gospel of peace; Above all, taking the shield of faith, wherewith ye shall be able to quench all the fiery darts of the wicked. And take the helmet of salvation, and the sword of the Spirit, which is the word of God: Praying always with all prayer and supplication in the Spirit, and watching thereunto with all perseverance and supplication for all saints.

– Ephesians 6:10–18

1662. No matter what you may be facing today, no matter your circumstances, leave your care in the hand of the Lord, for He cares for you. He will make it alright. He will work it out for your good. In that place of trust, you can truly say, "It Is Well With My Soul".

Come unto me, all ye that labour and are heavy laden, and I will give you rest. Take my yoke upon you, and learn of me; for I am meek and lowly in heart: and ye shall find rest unto your souls. For my yoke is easy, and my burden is light.

– Matthew 11:28–30

1663. Wisdom is not knowledge. Wisdom is developed or given. Knowledge must be pursued. Wise is the person who discerns that he or she needs more knowledge, and has the discipline to get it, and to use it to achieve the desired purposes.

Wisdom is the principal thing; therefore get wisdom: and with all thy getting get understanding.

– Proverbs 4:7

1664. In financial decisions, the bottom line is the *bottom line*. Decide based on the bottom line. If taking from your bottom line to give to someone else's bottom line causes your bottom line to grow, then do it. Always decide based on the bottom line. The bottom line is the *bottom line*.

A feast is made for laughter, and wine maketh merry: but money answereth all things.

> – Ecclesiastes 10:19

1665. We all have some "loose ends" that we haven't been able to *pin down* yet. None of us have it all together. Even those that we pay to *know*, have areas in their lives that are still like a *string hanging in the wind*. We're all walking by faith, whether we call it that or not. We're all pursuing an unseen *hope* of a higher perfection and better outcome.

The rich and the poor have this in common: the Lord made them both.

> – Proverbs 22:2

> Common English Bible (CEB)

1666. The future is in your hands. So, manage it well. What you do today will greatly impact tomorrow's outcomes.

Be not deceived; God is not mocked: for whatsoever a man soweth, that shall he also reap. For he that soweth to his flesh shall of the flesh reap corruption; but he that soweth to the Spirit shall of the Spirit reap life everlasting. And let us not be weary in well doing: for in due season we shall reap, if we faint not. As we have therefore opportunity, let us do good unto all men, especially unto them who are of the household of faith.

> – Galatians 6:7–10

1667. One speaker asked the question, "Would you rather have 20 half carat diamonds, or one 10 carat diamond?" I say, "I'll take both. I'll take the Tiffany's approach, and the Zale's approach." Leave no value on the table. Everything has value when properly marketed.

Cast thy bread upon the waters: for thou shalt find it after many days. Give a portion to seven, and also to eight; for thou knowest not what evil shall be upon the earth. If the clouds be full of rain, they empty themselves upon the earth: and if the tree fall toward the south, or toward the north, in the place where the tree falleth, there it shall be. He that observeth the wind shall not sow; and he that regardeth the clouds shall not reap. As thou knowest not what is the way of the spirit, nor how the bones do grow in the womb of her that is with child: even so thou knowest not the works of God who maketh all. In the morning sow thy seed, and in the evening withhold not thine hand: for thou knowest not whether shall prosper, either this or that, or whether they both shall be alike good.

– Ecclesiastes 11:1–6

1668. Marketing makes the revenue wheel go round!

The prophet that hath a dream, let him tell a dream; and he that hath my word, let him speak my word faithfully. What is the chaff to the wheat? saith the Lord. Is not my word like as a fire? saith the Lord; and like a hammer that breaketh the rock in pieces?

– Jeremiah 23:28–29

1669. The undeniable evidence of Jesus's resurrection lives inside of the spirit of every born–again believer. There's no denying the evidence of His resurrection, because we all know we have been changed from faith to faith, from glory to glory, and from strength to strength, purely from our unfeigned faith in His love and precious blood, which washed our sins away! Have a blessed Resurrection Sunday!

For God so loved the world, that he gave his only begotten Son, that whosoever believeth in him should not perish, but have everlasting life. For God sent not his Son into the world to condemn the world; but that the world through him might be saved.

– John 3:16–17

For whosoever shall call upon the name of the Lord shall be saved.

– Romans 10:13

1670. If you set big goals, you'll accomplish big things. If you set small goals, you'll accomplish small things. If you set no goals, you'll accomplish *nothing*.

And they said, Go to, let us build us a city and a tower, whose top may reach unto heaven; and let us make us a name, lest we be scattered abroad upon the face of the whole earth. And the Lord came down to see the city and the tower, which the children of men builded. And the Lord said, Behold, the people is one, and they have all one language; and this they begin to do: and now nothing will be restrained from them, which they have imagined to do.

– Genesis 11:4–6

1671. People with purpose make the best students. You don't have to give them a reason to stay motivated, focused, and passionate.

And the man Jeroboam was a mighty man of valour: and Solomon seeing the young man that he was industrious, he made him ruler over all the charge of the house of Joseph.

–1 Kings 11:28

Seest thou a man diligent in his business? he shall stand before kings; he shall not stand before mean men.

– Proverbs 22:29

1672. I declare that a mighty wave of success has been rolling and rolling and rolling, and moving forward underneath the surface of your life, and it's about to break through the surface like a mighty wave of *a blessing tsunami*, rising above, and sweeping all poverty, despair, and lack away from you and your family, both now and in future generations! In Jesus name, amen.

So shall they fear the name of the Lord from the west, and his glory from the rising of the sun. When the enemy shall come in like a flood, the Spirit of the Lord shall lift up a standard against him.

–Isaiah 59:19

1673. The sign of a true entrepreneur is the ability to create great things out of limited resources.

Now faith is the substance of things hoped for, the evidence of things not seen. For by it the elders obtained a good report. Through faith we understand that the worlds were framed by the word of God, so that things which are seen were not made of things which do appear.

– Hebrews 11:1–3

1674. The key to maintaining our peace is to learn to live an uncomplicated life in the midst of a very complicated world. Jesus is the key to peace. Jesus is the answer for the world today.

Peace I leave with you, my peace I give unto you: not as the world giveth, give I unto you. Let not your heart be troubled, neither let it be afraid.

– John 14:27

1675. You must win the *inner battle* before you can win the outer battle.

I beseech you therefore, brethren, by the mercies of God, that ye present your bodies a living sacrifice, holy, acceptable unto God, which is your reasonable service. And be not conformed to this world: but be ye transformed by the renewing of your mind, that ye may prove what is that good, and acceptable, and perfect, will of God.

– Romans 12:1–2

1676. If you would like a fresh start to your mental day, take time to read five or ten chapters of one of the four gospels, Matthew, Mark, Luke, or John. Read it aloud, so that your spirit and mind will hear you saying it. You will find it to be refreshing! Exhaust your doubt, and refresh your faith! Try it! You'll like it!

That he might sanctify and cleanse it with the washing of water by the word.

– Ephesians 5:26

1677. I'm too big now to be afraid of the *"boogie man"*. Intimidation practices don't work on me.

And in nothing terrified by your adversaries: which is to them an evident token of perdition, but to you of salvation, and that of God.

– Philippians 1:28

1678. A *talking* woman is a sign of good health. A *quiet* woman is a sign that something may be wrong.

She openeth her mouth with wisdom; and in her tongue is the law of kindness.

– Proverbs 31:26

1679. If on your journey of faith it seems like God has been leading you, yet, you haven't been reaching the place of success that you desire; well, that's exactly what He's doing. He's leading you to take the *next* step to success. Success takes steps. Success is a journey. Yet, if you keep taking the necessary steps, you will reach that place of success and fulfillment.

The steps of a good man are ordered by the Lord: and he delighteth in his way.

– Psalm 37:23

In the morning sow thy seed, and in the evening withhold not thine hand: for thou knowest not whether shall prosper, either this or that, or whether they both shall be alike good.

– Ecclesiastes 11:6

1680. One word from God can open your eyes from being *"future–blind"* and almost hopeless, to being passionately focused and hopeful for your future.

He answered and said, Whether he be a sinner or no, I know not: one thing I know, that, whereas I was blind, now I see.

– John 9:25

1681. Faith is admirable.

And it came to pass on a certain day, as he was teaching, that there were Pharisees and doctors of the law sitting by, which were come out of every town of Galilee, and Judaea, and Jerusalem: and the power of the Lord was present to heal them. And, behold, men brought in a bed a man which was taken with a palsy: and they sought means to bring him in, and to lay him before him. And when they could not find by what way they might bring him in because of the multitude, they went upon the housetop, and let him down through the tiling with his couch into the midst before Jesus. And when he saw their faith, he said unto him, Man, thy sins are forgiven thee. And the scribes and the Pharisees began to reason, saying, Who is this which speaketh blasphemies? Who can forgive sins, but God alone? But when Jesus perceived their thoughts, he answering said unto them, What reason ye in your hearts? Whether is easier, to say, Thy sins be forgiven thee; or to say, Rise up and walk? But that ye may know that the Son of man hath power upon earth to forgive sins, (he said unto the sick of the palsy,) I say unto thee, Arise, and take up thy couch, and go into thine house. And immediately he rose up before them, and took up that whereon he lay, and departed to his own house, glorifying God.

– Luke 5:17–25

1682. As a destiny person, your destiny is complete as soon as you make a decision to pursue it. You're not creating the destiny. You just decided to *pursue* it, and when you decided, it is done. All you must do is take the necessary steps. "It is *finished*."

After this, Jesus knowing that all things were now accomplished, that the scripture might be fulfilled, saith, I thirst. Now there was set a vessel full of vinegar: and they filled a spunge with vinegar, and put it upon hyssop, and put it to his mouth. When Jesus therefore had received the vinegar, he said, It is finished: and he bowed his head, and gave up the ghost.

– John 19:28–30

1683. If your money doesn't have a specific place to go, it will *go*.

Be thou diligent to know the state of thy flocks, and look well to thy herds. For riches are not for ever: and doth the crown endure to every generation? The hay appeareth, and the tender grass sheweth itself, and herbs of the mountains are gathered. The lambs are for thy clothing, and the goats are the price of the field. And thou shalt have goats milk enough for thy food, for the food of thy household, and for the maintenance for thy maidens.

– Proverbs 27:23–27

Wilt thou set thine eyes upon that which is not? for riches certainly make themselves wings; they fly away as an eagle toward heaven.

– Proverbs 23:5

1684. Ask people nicely, and they will do more for you so much easier.

A soft answer turneth away wrath: but grievous words stir up anger.

– Proverbs 15:1

1685. Once you reach a certain level of maturity, God expects you to rule yourself. He expects you to rule your own time, eating habits, work habits, and all areas of your life. That takes courage and commitment. However, you were born to rule and born again to reign.

Go to the ant, thou sluggard; consider her ways, and be wise: which having no guide, overseer, or ruler, provideth her meat in the summer, and gathereth her food in the harvest.

– Proverbs 6:6–8

1686. I command healing to your physical body and soul from every sickness, disease, infirmity, and weakness. You are now relieved from your affliction. Go forth in freedom, strength, and health. Jesus is your healer. The work is complete. In Jesus name, amen. Now, say, "I accept it by faith. In Jesus name, amen" It is done.

He sent his word, and healed them, and delivered them from their destructions.

– Psalm 107:20

1687. The greatest teachers are profitable practitioners of their lessons learned. They are proof positive of their wisdom gained.

The crown of the wise is their riches: but the foolishness of fools is folly.

– Proverbs 14:24

1688. Grease the wheels of hospitality with a gift. When you visit someone's home or city, bring a gift. Grease the wheels of hospitality with a gift.

A gift is as a precious stone in the eyes of him that hath it: whithersoever it turneth, it prospereth.

– Proverbs 17:8

1689. *Opportunity* is a walking Man. If you don't stop Him to sit down and have dinner, and to hear Him speak, He will keep walking on by.

Now, therefore hearken unto me, O ye children: for blessed are they that keep my ways. Hear instruction, and be wise, and refuse it not. Blessed is the man that heareth me, watching daily at my gates, waiting at the posts of my doors. For whoso findeth me findeth life, and shall obtain favour of the Lord. But he that sinneth against me wrongeth his own soul: all they that hate me love death.

– Proverbs 8:32–36

Now it came to pass, as they went, that he entered into a certain village: and a certain woman named Martha received him into her house. And she had a sister called Mary, which also sat at Jesus feet, and heard his word. But Martha was cumbered about much serving, and came to him, and said, Lord, dost thou not care that my sister hath left me to serve alone? bid her therefore that she help me. And Jesus answered and said unto her, Martha, Martha, thou art careful and troubled about many things: But one thing is needful: and Mary hath chosen that good part, which shall not be taken away from her.

– Luke 10:38–42

1690. I've been an escort to the debutante ball. I've been a date to the senior prom. But, most importantly I've been a happy groom at the altar for my wedding to my beautiful wife!

Whoso findeth a wife findeth a good thing, and obtaineth favour of the Lord.

– Proverbs 18:22

1691. God prepares you for life. If you keep on walking by faith, you'll be prepared for the next *leg of the race.*

A man's heart deviseth his way: but the Lord directeth his steps.

– Proverbs 16:9

1692. Go with the *flow of favor* in life, because you don't know what the future will hold. You will need it. Go with the flow of favor. Do the right thing when it's the right time, and you will have the right harvest at the right time.

He that diligently seeketh good procureth favour: but he that seeketh mischief, it shall come unto him.

– Proverbs 11:27

1693. Regarding the salvation appeal, make the appeal appealing, and not condemning. Make it appetizing to those who do not know Jesus, so that they will be interested enough to take advantage of the salvation offer.

For God so loved the world, that he gave his only begotten Son, that whosoever believeth in him should not perish, but have everlasting life. For God sent not his Son into the world to condemn the world; but that the world through him might be saved.

– John 3:16–17

1694. The greatest thing that you can do for your family is to be successful. Abraham had to leave his family to go and succeed. Isaac succeeded. Jacob went and succeeded. The greatest thing that you can do for your family is to be successful.

Now the Lord had said unto Abram, Get thee out of thy country, and from thy kindred, and from thy father's house,

unto a land that I will shew thee: And I will make of thee a
great nation, and I will bless thee, and make thy name great;
and thou shalt be a blessing: And I will bless them that bless
thee, and curse him that curseth thee: and in thee shall all
families of the earth be blessed. So Abram departed, as
the Lord had spoken unto him; and Lot went with him: and
Abram was seventy and five years old when he departed out
of Haran. And Abram took Sarai his wife, and Lot his
brother's son, and all their substance that they had gathered,
and the souls that they had gotten in Haran; and they went
forth to go into the land of Canaan; and into the land of
Canaan they came.

– Genesis 12:1–5

1695. We have completed the first portion of the year.
Have you set goals? Have you achieved your goals? Do you
need to set new goals? Do you need to recommit to your
goals? Goals are the key to achievement. You still have time in
the year to achieve great goals! You can do it! Set goals today!

And the Lord answered me, and said, Write the vision, and
make it plain upon tables, that he may run that readeth it. For
the vision is yet for an appointed time, but at the end it shall
speak, and not lie: though it tarry, wait for it; because it will
surely come, it will not tarry. Behold, his soul which is lifted
up is not upright in him: but the just shall live by his faith.

– Habakkuk 2:2–4

1696. In life, the people who walk in love walk the longest. Mother Teresa, Dr. Billy Graham, Dr. Norman Vincent Peale, the Apostle John, each of their lifestyles reflect the practice of walking in love, and they walked the longest in life. It's not miracles that keep you alive. It's your true, sincere love–walk. Many profess to walk in love, however, sincere love (free from hypocrisy, partiality, or duplicity) is tangible and apparent to even the most simplistic observer. True love can be seen, felt, and experienced. It will help you stay alive longer.

But ye, beloved, building up yourselves on your most holy faith, praying in the Holy Ghost, Keep yourselves in the love of God, looking for the mercy of our Lord Jesus Christ unto eternal life.

– Jude 20–21

1697. Sometimes it's all about practicality, rather than formality.

On the morrow, as they went on their journey, and drew nigh unto the city, Peter went up upon the housetop to pray about the sixth hour: And he became very hungry, and would have eaten: but while they made ready, he fell into a trance, And saw heaven opened, and a certain vessel descending upon him, as it had been a great sheet knit at the four corners, and let down to the earth: Wherein were all manner of fourfooted beasts of the earth, and wild beasts, and creeping things, and fowls of the air. And there came a voice to him, Rise, Peter; kill, and eat. But Peter said, Not so, Lord; for I have never eaten any thing that is common or unclean. And the voice spake unto him again the second time, What God hath cleansed, that call not thou common.

– Acts 10:9–15

1698. Christians without the fruit of the spirit are just as confusing to the world as *"Chamomile 5–hour Energy."*

Now the works of the flesh are manifest, which are these; Adultery, fornication, uncleanness, lasciviousness, Idolatry, witchcraft, hatred, variance, emulations, wrath, strife, seditions, heresies, Envyings, murders, drunkenness, revellings, and such like: of the which I tell you before, as I have also told you in time past, that they which do such things shall not inherit the kingdom of God. But the fruit of the Spirit is love, joy, peace, longsuffering, gentleness, goodness, faith, Meekness, temperance: against such there is no law. And they that are Christ's have crucified the flesh with the affections and lusts. If we live in the Spirit, let us also walk in the Spirit.

– Galatians 5:19–25

1699. We don't have to be threatened by artificial intelligence, which was programmed by human intelligence, which was imparted by Divine intelligence.

But thou, O Daniel, shut up the words, and seal the book, even to the time of the end: many shall run to and fro, and knowledge shall be increased.

– Daniel 12:4

1700. Regarding doing the work of God, prepare like it all depended on you, but seek God like it all depended on Him.

The preparations of the heart in man, and the answer of the tongue, is from the Lord.

– Proverbs 16:1

1701. You may feel like you need to make more money, but if you focus on making more progress, you will make more money.

Beloved, I wish above all things that thou mayest prosper and be in health, even as thy soul prospereth.

–3 John 2

1702. If along the *"song of life"* you've seemed to come across a low note, then, keep playing along and stringing along, because you're sure to be coming up on a *high note* soon!

The Lord is the portion of mine inheritance and of my cup: thou maintainest my lot. The lines are fallen unto me in pleasant places; yea, I have a goodly heritage. I will bless the Lord, who hath given me counsel: my reins also instruct me in the night seasons. I have set the Lord always before me: because he is at my right hand, I shall not be moved. Therefore my heart is glad, and my glory rejoiceth: my flesh also shall rest in hope. For thou wilt not leave my soul in hell; neither wilt thou suffer thine Holy One to see corruption. Thou wilt shew me the path of life: in thy presence is fulness of joy; at thy right hand there are pleasures for evermore.

– Psalm 16:5–11

1703. No matter how comfortable Christians become with the world in today's environment, don't forget that this is not a *Sunday morning picnic*. As long as you're working with *wolves*, no matter how they look like sheep, eventually, *the teeth and claws* will show up. Never forget that your great commission is to let your light so shine, so as to convert the world, and create disciples, rather than to ignore the need for change.

Love not the world, neither the things that are in the world. If any man love the world, the love of the Father is not in him. For all that is in the world, the lust of the flesh, and the lust of the eyes, and the pride of life, is not of the Father, but is of the world. And the world passeth away, and the lust thereof: but he that doeth the will of God abideth for ever. Little children, it is the last time: and as ye have heard that antichrist shall come, even now are there many antichrists; whereby we know that it is the last time. They went out from us, but they were not of us; for if they had been of us, they would no doubt have continued with us: but they went out, that they might be made manifest that they were not all of us. But ye have an unction from the Holy One, and ye know all things. I have not written unto you because ye know not the truth, but because ye know it, and that no lie is of the truth. Who is a liar but he that denieth that Jesus is the Christ? He is antichrist, that denieth the Father and the Son. Whosoever denieth the Son, the same hath not the Father: he that acknowledgeth the Son hath the Father also. Let that therefore abide in you, which ye have heard from the beginning. If that which ye have heard from the beginning shall remain in you, ye also shall continue in the Son, and in the Father. And this is the promise that he hath promised us, even eternal life. These things have I written unto you concerning them that seduce you. But the anointing which ye have received of him abideth in you, and ye need not that any man teach you: but as the same anointing teacheth you of all things, and is truth, and is no lie, and even as it hath taught you, ye shall abide in him. And now, little children, abide in him; that, when he shall appear, we may have confidence, and not be ashamed before him at his coming. If ye know that he is righteous, ye know that every one that doeth righteousness is born of him.

–1 John 2:15–29

1704. Christianity is inclusive and *exclusive*. The "Door" is open to whosoever will believe. The *Blessing* is available only to those who obey God's Word. Christianity is inclusive and exclusive, at the same time.

For God so loved the world, that he gave his only begotten Son, that whosoever believeth in him should not perish, but have everlasting life. For God sent not his Son into the world to condemn the world; but that the world through him might be saved.

– John 3:16–17

If ye be willing and obedient, ye shall eat the good of the land.

– Isaiah 1:19

1705. You will always win a battle if you keep your peace.

And Jesus stood before the governor: and the governor asked him, saying, Art thou the King of the Jews? And Jesus said unto him, Thou sayest. And when he was accused of the chief priests and elders, he answered nothing. Then said Pilate unto him, Hearest thou not how many things they witness against thee? And he answered him to never a word; insomuch that the governor marvelled greatly.

– Matthew 27:11–14

1706. Keep your head up. Walk like a king. Stay up and never slide down. Be the victor and not the victim. And never let anybody put you on the *back of the bus*!

Let no man despise thy youth; but be thou an example of the believers, in word, in conversation, in charity, in spirit, in faith, in purity.

–1 Timothy 4:12

And as they bound him with thongs, Paul said unto the centurion that stood by, Is it lawful for you to scourge a man that is a Roman, and uncondemned? When the centurion heard that, he went and told the chief captain, saying, Take heed what thou doest: for this man is a Roman. Then the chief captain came, and said unto him, Tell me, art thou a Roman? He said, Yea. And the chief captain answered, With a great sum obtained I this freedom. And Paul said, But I was free born. Then straightway they departed from him which should have examined him: and the chief captain also was afraid, after he knew that he was a Roman, and because he had bound him. On the morrow, because he would have known the certainty wherefore he was accused of the Jews, he loosed him from his bands, and commanded the chief priests and all their council to appear, and brought Paul down, and set him before them.

– Acts 22:25–30

1707. Respect for yourself and others will make for a respectable relationship.

The rich and poor meet together: the Lord is the maker of them all.

– Proverbs 22:2

1708. Here's a lesson: Never miss an opportunity to be a blessing to others, even when it takes courage to say something or to do something. Always choose to be a blessing to others.

Be not deceived; God is not mocked: for whatsoever a man soweth, that shall he also reap. For he that soweth to his flesh shall of the flesh reap corruption; but he that soweth to the

Spirit shall of the Spirit reap life everlasting. And let us not be weary in well doing: for in due season we shall reap, if we faint not. As we have therefore opportunity, let us do good unto all men, especially unto them who are of the household of faith.

– Galatians 6:7–10

1709. Faith comes by hearing. Faith is the ability to take action. If you have not been taking enough action in life, you must take time to build up your faith, by listening to things that can help build up your motivation to take action. Faith comes by hearing. Faith is the ability to take action.

So then faith cometh by hearing, and hearing by the word of God.

– Romans 10:17

1710. God sends us undeniable signs of His notable favor! Our faith should be in His unchanging Word in the Bible. Yet, He created the whole wide world, He can use what He wants to show us signs of notable favor!

I do set my bow in the cloud, and it shall be for a token of a covenant between me and the earth. And it shall come to pass, when I bring a cloud over the earth, that the bow shall be seen in the cloud: And I will remember my covenant, which is between me and you and every living creature of all flesh; and the waters shall no more become a flood to destroy all flesh. And the bow shall be in the cloud; and I will look upon it, that

I may remember the everlasting covenant between God and every living creature of all flesh that is upon the earth. And God said unto Noah, This is the token of the covenant, which I have established between me and all flesh that is upon the earth.

– Genesis 9:13–17

1711. A *will* to live will help you live.

I call heaven and earth to record this day against you, that I have set before you life and death, blessing and cursing: therefore choose life, that both thou and thy seed may live.

– Deuteronomy 30:19

1712. Creation is the first phase of profit. You can always sell something that you have. You can't sell something that you don't have. Creation is the first phase of profit.

Now therefore perform the doing of it; that as there was a readiness to will, so there may be a performance also out of that which ye have. For if there be first a willing mind, it is accepted according to that a man hath, and not according to that he hath not.

–2 Corinthians 8:11–12

1713. Nobody is concerned about doing what you need to do, but you. If you don't do it, it won't get done. If you don't run your race, it won't be run. Nobody is concerned about you, and what you need to do, but you.

But let every man prove his own work, and then shall he have rejoicing in himself alone, and not in another.

– Galatians 6:4

1714. Do big things and you will become larger. Do even *more* big things, and you will become larger even *faster*.

And Jesus increased in wisdom and stature, and in favour with God and man.

– Luke 2:52

1715. Knowledge comes from learning and study. Growing comes from *doing*.

And Jesus increased in wisdom and stature, and in favour with God and man.

– Luke 2:52

1716. When life becomes confusing, pray in the Holy Ghost. Pray out the answers to those *mysteries*.

For he that speaketh in an unknown tongue speaketh not unto men, but unto God: for no man understandeth him; howbeit in the spirit he speaketh mysteries.

–1 Corinthians 14:2

1717. What would history be called if women ruled the world? It would be called *her–story!*

Many daughters have done virtuously, but thou excellest them all. Favour is deceitful, and beauty is vain: but a woman that feareth the Lord, she shall be praised. Give her of the fruit of her hands; and let her own works praise her in the gates.

– Proverbs 31:29–31

1718. Don't listen to *"loser talk"*, even if it's coming from a winner. Rather, pay attention to what the winner is doing and follow their *example*, and you'll become a winner too. Some people tell you to "take it easy and relax", and "don't worry, be happy" and to "trust and believe" and everything will come to you in time. However, they know the truth. Everything they have obtained and maintain is by hard work and effort. Do the things that winners do, and not just what they say, and you will become a winner *too.*

Even so faith, if it hath not works, is dead, being alone. Yea, a man may say, Thou hast faith, and I have works: shew me thy faith without thy works, and I will shew thee my faith by my works.

– James 2:17–18

1719. Regarding sales, continue to create excellence, and be productive, rather than overly focusing on the sales process. You can always sell something that you have, but you can't sell something that you don't have. Therefore, focus on being productive and excellent, just like every successful innovator, and then the sales process will be able to be taken care of on its own.

But rather seek ye the kingdom of God; and all these things shall be added unto you. Fear not, little flock; for it is your Fathers good pleasure to give you the kingdom. Sell that ye have, and give alms; provide yourselves bags which wax not old, a treasure in the heavens that faileth not, where no thief approacheth, neither moth corrupteth. For where your treasure is, there will your heart be also.

– Luke 12:31–34

1720. Close the circle of productivity with *profit*.

Now therefore perform the doing of it; that as there was a readiness to will, so there may be a performance also out of that which ye have. For if there be first a willing mind, it is accepted according to that a man hath, and not according to that he hath not.

–2 Corinthians 8:11–12

1721. Favor *plus* labor equals success.

In all labour there is profit: but the talk of the lips tendeth only to penury.

– Proverbs 14:23

1722. Success may be slow, but success is sure, if you keep working on the right things in the right way overtime. Success may be slow, but success is sure.

In the morning sow thy seed, and in the evening withhold not thine hand: for thou knowest not whether shall prosper, either this or that, or whether they both shall be alike good.

– Ecclesiastes 11:6

1723. Life takes *faith* and *trust*. It takes faith to go forward, and trust to be patient in the process.

That ye be not slothful, but followers of them who through faith and patience inherit the promises.

– Hebrews 6:12

1724. May you demonstrate the *style of a victor*, and not a victim: a winner and not a *whiner*. Greater is He who is in you, than he that is in the world. And if God be for you, who can be against you?

For though we walk in the flesh, we do not war after the flesh: (For the weapons of our warfare are not carnal, but mighty through God to the pulling down of strong holds;) Casting down imaginations, and every high thing that exalteth itself against the knowledge of God, and bringing into captivity every thought to the obedience of Christ.

–2 Corinthians 10:3–5

1725. A life built upon truth *appreciates* in value over time. A life built upon falsehood declines and *depreciates* in value over time.

The memory of the just is blessed: but the name of the wicked shall rot.

– Proverbs 10:7

1726. Patience and planning are the keys to financial freedom. Impatience and impulsiveness are the keys to continued poverty.

Also, that the soul be without knowledge, it is not good; and he that hasteth with his feet sinneth.

– Proverbs 19:2

Wisdom is good with an inheritance: and by it there is profit to them that see the sun. For wisdom is a defence, and money is a defence: but the excellency of knowledge is, that wisdom giveth life to them that have it.

– Ecclesiastes 7:11–12

1727. There are many thoughts that may go through your mind about what you had to do today, but what you actually had to do, you did it. Each day must stand on its on.

Take therefore no thought for the morrow: for the morrow shall take thought for the things of itself. Sufficient unto the day is the evil thereof.

– Matthew 6:34

1728. Become comfortable with being great. Come out of your comfort zone. Even a turtle will stick its neck out when it becomes comfortable. If you do, you may be surprised and realize that you are a *giraffe!*

Thou shalt increase my greatness, and comfort me on every side.

– Psalm 71:21

1729. Take time to meditate and confess God's Word over every area of your life. Allow God's Word to pierce through the darkness. Do not let your vision of the future be suffocated by circumstances. Rather, pierce through the darkness with God's Word.

For the word of God is quick, and powerful, and sharper than any twoedged sword, piercing even to the dividing asunder of soul and spirit, and of the joints and marrow, and is a discerner of the thoughts and intents of the heart. Neither is there any creature that is not manifest in his sight: but all things are naked and opened unto the eyes of him with whom we have to do. Seeing then that we have a great high priest, that is passed into the heavens, Jesus the Son of God, let us hold fast our profession. For we have not an high priest which cannot be touched with the feeling of our infirmities; but was in all points tempted like as we are, yet without sin. Let us therefore come boldly unto the throne of grace, that we may obtain mercy, and find grace to help in time of need.

– Hebrews 4:12–16

1730. The eyes are the windows to the soul. Be careful of what you allow into the house. It could be darkness, or it could be light. One will blind your purpose. The other will enlighten your way. The eyes are the windows to the soul. Be careful of what you allow in the house.

The light of the body is the eye: if therefore thine eye be single, thy whole body shall be full of light. But if thine eye be evil, thy whole body shall be full of darkness. If therefore the light that is in thee be darkness, how great is that darkness!

– Matthew 6:22–23

My son, attend to my words; incline thine ear unto my sayings. Let them not depart from thine eyes; keep them in the midst of thine heart. For they are life unto those that find them, and health to all their flesh. Keep thy heart with all diligence; for out of it are the issues of life. Put away from thee a froward mouth, and perverse lips put far from thee. Let thine eyes look right on, and let thine eyelids look straight before thee. Ponder the path of thy feet, and let all thy ways be established. Turn not to the right hand nor to the left: remove thy foot from evil.

– Proverbs 4:20–27

1731. The "good fight of faith" that you have been in is preparation for the next level. God can't let you be a *wimp* when you're destined to become "the head and not the tail." You've got to be tough to be *"large and in charge!"*

Fight the good fight of faith, lay hold on eternal life, whereunto thou art also called, and hast professed a good profession before many witnesses.

–1 Timothy 6:12

1732. If you focus on saving money, you will save a lot of money. If you focus on spending money, you will spend a lot of money. *Focus* is the key to financial freedom or financial poverty.

Be thou diligent to know the state of thy flocks, and look well to thy herds. For riches are not for ever: and doth the crown endure to every generation? The hay appeareth, and the tender grass sheweth itself, and herbs of the mountains are gathered. The lambs are for thy clothing, and the goats are the price of the field. And thou shalt have goats milk enough for thy food, for the food of thy household, and for the maintenance for thy maidens.

– Proverbs 27:23–27

1733. Average people will often try to judge above average people in order to bring them down to their level.

It pleased Darius to set over the kingdom an hundred and twenty princes, which should be over the whole kingdom; And over these three presidents; of whom Daniel was first: that the princes might give accounts unto them, and the king should have no damage. Then this Daniel was preferred above the presidents and princes, because an excellent spirit was in him; and the king thought to set him over the whole realm. Then the presidents and princes sought to find occasion against Daniel concerning the kingdom; but they could find none occasion nor fault; forasmuch as he was faithful, neither was there any error or fault found in him. Then said these men, We shall not find any occasion against this Daniel, except we find it against him concerning the law of his God.

– Daniel 6:1–5

1734. People who *get it done* like to work with people who get it done.

Even so faith, if it hath not works, is dead, being alone. Yea, a man may say, Thou hast faith, and I have works: shew me thy faith without thy works, and I will shew thee my faith by my works.

– James 2:17–18

1735. Concerning problems in life, after the *eggs are cracked*, you might as well go ahead and make an *omelette.*

And we know that all things work together for good to them that love God, to them who are the called according to his purpose. For whom he did foreknow, he also did predestinate to be conformed to the image of his Son, that he might be the firstborn among many brethren.

– Romans 8:28–29

1736. Giving says more about the giver than it does about the receiver.

I have shewed you all things, how that so labouring ye ought to support the weak, and to remember the words of the Lord Jesus, how he said, It is more blessed to give than to receive.

– Acts 20:35

1737. Both fear and faith are *alternate states of reality*. Take time to dwell in the alternate state of faith, and you will change your reality. Avoid fear, because it is not a place that you want to be in. Choose faith and you will change your reality.

I sought the Lord, and he heard me, and delivered me from all my fears.

– Psalm 34:4

1738. When it's time for your blessing, God can *compress* time to get it to you. Time is not a factor when it's time for your blessing. When you're ready, God will get you there.

And the angel of the Lord spake unto Philip, saying, Arise, and go toward the south unto the way that goeth down from

Jerusalem unto Gaza, which is desert. And he arose and went: and, behold, a man of Ethiopia, an eunuch of great authority under Candace queen of the Ethiopians, who had the charge of all her treasure, and had come to Jerusalem for to worship, Was returning, and sitting in his chariot read Esaias the prophet. Then the Spirit said unto Philip, Go near, and join thyself to this chariot. And Philip ran thither to him, and heard him read the prophet Esaias, and said, Understandest thou what thou readest? And he said, How can I, except some man should guide me? And he desired Philip that he would come up and sit with him. The place of the scripture which he read was this, He was led as a sheep to the slaughter; and like a lamb dumb before his shearer, so opened he not his mouth: In his humiliation his judgment was taken away: and who shall declare his generation? for his life is taken from the earth. And the eunuch answered Philip, and said, I pray thee, of whom speaketh the prophet this? of himself, or of some other man? Then Philip opened his mouth, and began at the same scripture, and preached unto him Jesus. And as they went on their way, they came unto a certain water: and the eunuch said, See, here is water; what doth hinder me to be baptized? And Philip said, If thou believest with all thine heart, thou mayest. And he answered and said, I believe that Jesus Christ is the Son of God. And he commanded the chariot to stand still: and they went down both into the water, both Philip and the eunuch; and he baptized him. And when they were come up out of the water, the Spirit of the Lord caught away Philip, that the eunuch saw him no more: and he went on his way rejoicing. But Philip was found at Azotus: and passing through he preached in all the cities, till he came to Caesarea.

– Acts 8:26–40

1739. The only difference between those with an education, and those without an education, is that those with an education have been put in an environment where they have had to successfully prove their ability in a specific area. If you do not have an education, then you must take on that opportunity for yourself, and prove it profitably. Many notable people have done it before you. If you can do that, then, it doesn't make a substantial difference. However, it's best to *stack the deck* in your favor by taking advantage of every possible educational opportunity.

Also, that the soul be without knowledge, it is not good; and he that hasteth with his feet sinneth.

– Proverbs 19:2

Wisdom is good with an inheritance: and by it there is profit to them that see the sun. For wisdom is a defence, and money is a defence: but the excellency of knowledge is, that wisdom giveth life to them that have it.

– Ecclesiastes 7:11–12

1740. This week, God is going to give you moments with Him that He hasn't shared with any other person in all of eternity. The moments will be with just you and Him. They will be moments of the *supernatural*. If you expect them and recognize them when they come, you will see even more of them.

But as it is written, Eye hath not seen, nor ear heard, neither have entered into the heart of man, the things which God hath prepared for them that love him.

–1 Corinthians 2:9

1741. There's no conundrum or challenge in your life that someone else hasn't faced in some form or fashion before you. The answer is inside of the Bible. It may be in another book, another person, or inside of *your* spirit. You can draw it out through prayer, study, research, and relationships. You can find the answer. It's available!

The thing that hath been, it is that which shall be; and that which is done is that which shall be done: and there is no new thing under the sun.

– Ecclesiastes 1:9

Buy the truth, and sell it not; also wisdom, and instruction, and understanding.

– Proverbs 23:23

1742. There's nothing worse than *bourgeoisie* people treating others with disesteem, because they deem them lower than themselves or less educated than themselves. Truly wealthy people should have the wisdom to highly esteem and appreciate all people. We all are dependent upon the other. The rich depend upon the resources of the poor in order to stay rich. The poor depend upon the systems of the wealthy in order to function in life. We are all interdependent.

The rich and poor meet together: the Lord is the maker of them all.

– Proverbs 22:2

1743. When a man's ways please the Lord, He will make both enemies and "frenemies" to be at peace with you! God will showcase you as a sign of His extraordinary favor and goodness! All they will be able say is, "God has sure been good to you!" And, all you can is "Sho'nuf! You're right! Praise God!"

When the Lord turned again the captivity of Zion, we were like them that dream. Then was our mouth filled with laughter, and our tongue with singing: then said they among the heathen, The Lord hath done great things for them. The Lord hath done great things for us; whereof we are glad. Turn again our captivity, O Lord, as the streams in the south. They that sow in tears shall reap in joy. He that goeth forth and weepeth, bearing precious seed, shall doubtless come again with rejoicing, bringing his sheaves with him.

– Psalm 126

Shew me a token for good; that they which hate me may see it, and be ashamed: because thou, Lord, hast holpen me, and comforted me.

– Psalm 86:17

1744. God has enabled you. God has made you able. God has provided you with the means, opportunity, power, and authority to be successful. He's made it possible. Step out in faith. Use what you have, and success is guaranteed! God has given you wisdom and ability to prosper!

But thou shalt remember the Lord thy God: for it is he that giveth thee power to get wealth, that he may establish his covenant which he sware unto thy fathers, as it is this day.

– Deuteronomy 8:18

1745. A mother is smarter than just book knowledge. It's called "mother's wit!" Mothers are nurturers of destiny.

And it came to pass, that when Isaac was old, and his eyes were dim, so that he could not see, he called Esau his eldest son, and said unto him, My son: and he said unto him, Behold, here am I. And he said, Behold now, I am old, I know not the day of my death: Now therefore take, I pray thee, thy weapons, thy quiver and thy bow, and go out to the field, and take me some venison; And make me savoury meat, such as I love, and bring it to me, that I may eat; that my soul may bless thee before I die. And Rebekah heard when Isaac spake to Esau his son. And Esau went to the field to hunt for venison, and to bring it. And Rebekah spake unto Jacob her son, saying, Behold, I heard thy father speak unto Esau thy brother, saying, Bring me venison, and make me savoury meat, that I may eat, and bless thee before the Lord before my death. Now therefore, my son, obey my voice according to that which I command thee. Go now to the flock, and fetch me from thence two good kids of the goats; and I will make them savoury meat for thy father, such as he loveth: And thou shalt bring it to thy father, that he may eat, and that he may bless thee before his death. And Jacob said to Rebekah his mother, Behold, Esau my brother is a hairy man, and I am a smooth man: My father peradventure will feel me, and I shall seem to him as a deceiver; and I shall bring a curse upon me, and not a blessing. And his mother said unto him, Upon me be thy curse, my son: only obey my voice, and go fetch me them. And he went, and fetched, and brought them to his mother: and his mother made savoury meat, such as his father loved. And Rebekah took goodly raiment of her eldest son Esau, which were with her in the house, and put them upon Jacob her younger son: And she put the skins of the kids of the goats upon his hands, and upon the smooth of his neck: And she gave the savoury meat and the bread, which she had prepared, into the hand of her son Jacob. And he came unto his father, and said, My father: and he said, Here am I; who art thou, my son? And Jacob said unto his father, I am Esau thy first born; I have done according as thou badest me: arise, I pray thee, sit and eat of my venison, that thy soul may bless me. And Isaac said unto his son, How is it that thou hast found it so quickly, my son? And he said, Because the Lord thy God brought it to me. And Isaac said unto Jacob, Come near, I pray thee, that I may feel thee, my son, whether thou be my very son Esau or not. And Jacob went near unto Isaac his father; and he felt him, and said, The voice is Jacob's voice, but the hands are the hands of Esau. And he discerned him not, because his hands were hairy, as his brother Esau's hands: so he blessed him. And he said, Art thou my very son Esau? And he said, I am. And he said, Bring it near to me, and I will eat of my sons

venison, that my soul may bless thee. And he brought it near
to him, and he did eat: and he brought him wine and he drank.
And his father Isaac said unto him, Come near now, and kiss
me, my son. And he came near, and kissed him: and he
smelled the smell of his raiment, and blessed him, and said,
See, the smell of my son is as the smell of a field which
the Lord hath blessed: Therefore God give thee of the dew of
heaven, and the fatness of the earth, and plenty of corn and
wine: Let people serve thee, and nations bow down to thee: be
lord over thy brethren, and let thy mother's sons bow down
to thee: cursed be every one that curseth thee, and blessed be
he that blesseth thee.

– Genesis 27:1–29

1746. When we're led only by our feelings and act only
instinctively or impulsively, rather than by principles and
discernment, we may tend to do things that will have long-
term negative consequences. Also, things that go around have
a tendency to come back around, particularly, in relationships.

And Laban said unto Jacob, Because thou art my brother,
shouldest thou therefore serve me for nought? tell me, what
shall thy wages be? And Laban had two daughters: the name of
the elder was Leah, and the name of the younger was Rachel.
Leah was tender eyed; but Rachel was beautiful and well
favoured. And Jacob loved Rachel; and said, I will serve thee
seven years for Rachel thy younger daughter. And Laban said,
It is better that I give her to thee, than that I should give her to
another man: abide with me. And Jacob served seven years
for Rachel; and they seemed unto him but a few days, for the

love he had to her. And Jacob said unto Laban, Give me my wife, for my days are fulfilled, that I may go in unto her. And Laban gathered together all the men of the place, and made a feast. And it came to pass in the evening, that he took Leah his daughter, and brought her to him; and he went in unto her. And Laban gave unto his daughter Leah Zilpah his maid for an handmaid. And it came to pass, that in the morning, behold, it was Leah: and he said to Laban, What is this thou hast done unto me? did not I serve with thee for Rachel? wherefore then hast thou beguiled me? And Laban said, It must not be so done in our country, to give the younger before the firstborn. Fulfil her week, and we will give thee this also for the service which thou shalt serve with me yet seven other years. And Jacob did so, and fulfilled her week: and he gave him Rachel his daughter to wife also.

– Genesis 29:15–28

1747. Life takes prayer to get you there.

And he spake a parable unto them *to this end*, that men ought always to pray, and not to faint.

– Luke 18:1

1748. Exercise, healthy food, and rest help the body and mind deal with stress, so that you can do your best. It helps you recalibrate. It balances the chemicals in the body and brain. If you want to do your best, be sure to exercise, eat right, and get your rest.

And Ahab told Jezebel all that Elijah had done, and withal how he had slain all the prophets with the sword. Then Jezebel sent a messenger unto Elijah, saying, So let the gods do to me, and more also, if I make not thy life as the life of one of them by to morrow about this time. And when he saw that, he arose, and went for his life, and came to Beersheba, which belongeth to Judah, and left his servant there. But he himself went a days journey into the wilderness, and came and sat down under a juniper tree: and he requested for himself that he might die; and said, It is enough; now, O Lord, take away my life; for I am not better than my fathers. And as he lay and slept under a juniper tree, behold, then an angel touched him, and said unto him, Arise and eat. And he looked, and, behold, there was a cake baken on the coals, and a cruse of water at his head. And he did eat and drink, and laid him down again. And the angel of the Lord came again the second time, and touched him, and said, Arise and eat; because the journey is too great for thee. And he arose, and did eat and drink, and went in the strength of that meat forty days and forty nights unto Horeb the mount of God.

–1 Kings 19:1–8

1749. It takes self–control to have self–control.

He that answereth a matter before he heareth it, it is folly and shame unto him.

– Proverbs 18:13

The discretion of a man deferreth his anger; and it is his glory to pass over a transgression.

– Proverbs 19:11

1750. One disgruntled employee amongst many happy employees may say something about that employee. Several disgruntled employees working for a particular boss, may say something about that boss.

Servants, be obedient to them that are your masters according to the flesh, with fear and trembling, in singleness of your heart, as unto Christ; Not with eyeservice, as menpleasers; but as the servants of Christ, doing the will of God from the heart; With good will doing service, as to the Lord, and not to men: Knowing that whatsoever good thing any man doeth, the same shall he receive of the Lord, whether he be bond or free. And, ye masters, do the same things unto them, forbearing threatening: knowing that your Master also is in heaven; neither is there respect of persons with him.

– Ephesians 6:5–9

1751. Regarding relationships, when people are convinced of one another's love, they don't have to work as hard to keep one another fixed. Even if sometimes they may seem to be offended, they know that the other person's love will remain stable. People in relationships with others who are not as secure in their love will have to work harder to try to keep the other person fixed, because there's a certain amount of uncertainty. Often, these types of relationships are performance–based, rather than being based on *agape* love.

Can a woman forget her sucking child, that she should not have compassion on the son of her womb? yea, they may forget, yet will I not forget thee. Behold, I have graven thee upon the palms of my hands; thy walls are continually before me.

– Isaiah 49:15–16

And the third day there was a marriage in Cana of Galilee; and the mother of Jesus was there: And both Jesus was called, and his disciples, to the marriage. And when they wanted wine, the mother of Jesus saith unto him, They have no wine. Jesus saith unto her, Woman, what have I to do with thee? mine hour is not yet come. His mother saith unto the servants, Whatsoever he saith unto you, do it. And there were set there six waterpots of stone, after the manner of the purifying of the Jews, containing two or three firkins apiece. Jesus saith unto them, Fill the waterpots with water. And they filled them up to the brim. And he saith unto them, Draw out now, and bear unto the governor of the feast. And they bare it. When the ruler of the feast had tasted the water that was made wine, and knew not whence it was: (but the servants which drew the water knew;) the governor of the feast called the bridegroom, And saith unto him, Every man at the beginning doth set forth good wine; and when men have well drunk, then that which is worse: but thou hast kept the good wine until now. This beginning of miracles did Jesus in Cana of

Galilee, and manifested forth his glory; and his disciples believed on him.

– John 2:1–11

1752. The unwise and insecure live for the commendation of men. The wise and eternally secure live for the commendation of God.

Do we begin again to commend ourselves? or need we, as some others, epistles of commendation to you, or letters of commendation from you? Ye are our epistle written in our hearts, known and read of all men: Forasmuch as ye are manifestly declared to be the epistle of Christ ministered by us, written not with ink, but with the Spirit of the living God; not in tables of stone, but in fleshy tables of the heart.

–2 Corinthians 3:1–3

For we dare not make ourselves of the number, or compare ourselves with some that commend themselves: but they measuring themselves by themselves, and comparing themselves among themselves, are not wise.

–2 Corinthians 10:12

1753. You must do what's required to obtain what's desired. What's required usually is much more than what you at first anticipated.

For a dream cometh through the multitude of business; and a fools voice is known by multitude of words.

– Ecclesiastes 5:3

1754. You've lost perspective when you start to throw away good food just because you're full. You've lost perspective when you start to throw away good people, just because you're tired of them.

The full soul loatheth an honeycomb; but to the hungry soul every bitter thing is sweet.

– Proverbs 27:7

1755. Always be thinking *problem prevention*, and you'll avoid a lot of problems.

The beginning of strife is as when one letteth out water: therefore leave off contention, before it be meddled with.

– Proverbs 17:14

1756. The beginning of healthy relationships is at the casting out of fear.

But speaking the truth in love, may grow up into him in all things, which is the head, *even* Christ.

– Ephesians 4:15

There is no fear in love; but perfect love casteth out fear: because fear hath torment. He that feareth is not made perfect in love.

–1 John 4:18

1757. The worst thing a brother can do is to have the *sisters* against you. The best thing a brother can do is to have the sisters *for you.*

My son, keep my words, and lay up my commandments with thee. Keep my commandments, and live; and my law as the apple of thine eye. Bind them upon thy fingers, write them upon the table of thine heart. Say unto wisdom, Thou art my sister; and call understanding thy kinswoman: That they may keep thee from the strange woman, from the stranger which flattereth with her words.

–Proverbs 7:1–5

1758. *Judgment day* may take a longtime to come, but judgment day *always* comes.

But if ye will not do so, behold, ye have sinned against the Lord: and be sure your sin will find you out.

– Numbers 32:23

1759. Life is like a close race. The person who *leans in* will win. Lean in! Put your heart into the race!

Know ye not that they which run in a race run all, but one receiveth the prize? So run, that ye may obtain. And every man that striveth for the mastery is temperate in all things. Now they do it to obtain a corruptible crown; but we an incorruptible. I therefore so run, not as uncertainly; so fight I, not as one that beateth the air: But I keep under my body, and bring it into subjection: lest that by any means, when I have preached to others, I myself should be a castaway.

–1 Corinthians 9:24–27

1760. Some things are better unsaid.

The beginning of strife is as when one letteth out water: therefore leave off contention, before it be meddled with.

– Proverbs 17:14

1761. A good friend is not afraid to tell you the truth.

But speaking the truth in love, may grow up into him in all things, which is the head, *even* Christ.

– Ephesians 4:15

1762. Give honor to whom honor is due. Honor is an *earned asset* that has lasting value. Once you have done what's necessary to attain it, you must do all within your power to maintain it. Honor is a precious gift.

Wherefore the Lord God of Israel saith, I said indeed that thy house, and the house of thy father, should walk before me for ever: but now the Lord saith, Be it far from me; for them that honour me I will honour, and they that despise me shall be lightly esteemed.

−1 Samuel 2:30

1763. What's done in the dark will eventually come to the light.

But if ye will not do so, behold, ye have sinned against the Lord: and be sure your sin will find you out.

– Numbers 32:23

1764. Success is achievable. You can obtain it if you train for it. You must prepare for success. You must run the race to win. You must keep your eyes on the prize, and lay aside everything that hinders you in the race. Success is achievable. You were born to win. You were born to be a champion!

Know ye not that they which run in a race run all, but one receiveth the prize? So run, that ye may obtain. And every man that striveth for the mastery is temperate in all things. Now they do it to obtain a corruptible crown; but we an incorruptible. I therefore so run, not as uncertainly; so fight I, not as one that beateth the air: But I keep under my body, and bring it into subjection: lest that by any means, when I have preached to others, I myself should be a castaway.

−1 Corinthians 9:24−27

1765. Sometimes it's more glory for people to see you struggle and overcome, than to be able to act like you have no problems and fake people out. There's glory in your struggles.

For this thing I besought the Lord thrice, that it might depart from me. And he said unto me, My grace is sufficient for thee: for my strength is made perfect in weakness. Most gladly therefore will I rather glory in my infirmities, that the power of Christ may rest upon me.

–2 Corinthians 12:8–9

1766. The best meals have plenty of flavor without being overly filling. The best conversations have plenty of meaning without an overuse of words.

A word fitly spoken is like apples of gold in pictures of silver.

– Proverbs 25:11

Ointment and perfume rejoice the heart: so doth the sweetness of a man's friend by hearty counsel.

– Proverbs 27:9

1767. As you take care of others, be sure to take care of you, because no one will take care of you, like you're supposed to take care of you.

Jesus said unto him, Thou shalt love the Lord thy God with all thy heart, and with all thy soul, and with all thy mind. This is the first and great commandment. And the second is like unto it, Thou shalt love thy neighbour as thyself. On these two commandments hang all the law and the prophets.

– Matthew 22:37–40

1768. Never present a positive idea to a negative person. Else, it will be negatively impacted.

And they came unto the brook of Eshcol, and cut down from thence a branch with one cluster of grapes, and they bare it between two upon a staff; and they brought of the pomegranates, and of the figs. The place was called the brook Eshcol, because of the cluster of grapes which the children of Israel cut down from thence. And they returned from searching of the land after forty days. And they went and came to Moses, and to Aaron, and to all the congregation of the children of Israel, unto the wilderness of Paran, to Kadesh; and brought back word unto them, and unto all the congregation, and shewed them the fruit of the land. And they told him, and said, We came unto the land whither thou sentest us, and surely it floweth with milk and honey; and this is the fruit of it. Nevertheless the people be strong that dwell in the land, and the cities are walled, and very great: and moreover we saw the children of Anak there. The Amalekites dwell in the land of the south: and the Hittites, and the Jebusites, and the Amorites, dwell in the mountains: and the Canaanites dwell by the sea, and by the coast of Jordan. And Caleb stilled the people before Moses, and said, Let us go up at once, and possess it; for we are well able to overcome it. But the men that went up with him said, We be not able to go up against the people; for they are stronger than we. And they brought up an evil report of the land which they had searched unto the children of Israel, saying, The land, through which we have gone to search it, is a land that eateth up the inhabitants thereof; and all the people that we saw in it are men of a great stature. And there we saw the giants, the sons of Anak, which come of the giants: and we were in our own sight as grasshoppers, and so we were in their sight.

— Numbers 13:23–33

1769. You are an optimum, excellent, superior, outstanding, godly, exceptional person. You fulfill God's highest ideals. You're pleasing to God. He loves you very much. He wishes above all things that you prosper, and be in good health, even as your soul prospers. And He desires for you to have a long, exceptional, and fulfilling life. You are blessed.

I will praise thee; for I am fearfully and wonderfully made: marvellous are thy works; and that my soul knoweth right well.

— Psalm 139:14

1770. Listen to the customers, rather than listening to the experts. The customers are the experts.

Jesus saith unto them, My meat is to do the will of him that sent me, and to finish his work. Say not ye, There are yet four months, and then cometh harvest? behold, I say unto you, Lift up your eyes, and look on the fields; for they are white already to harvest. And he that reapeth receiveth wages, and gathereth fruit unto life eternal: that both he that soweth and he that reapeth may rejoice together. And herein is that saying true, One soweth, and another reapeth. I sent you to reap that whereon ye bestowed no labour: other men laboured, and ye are entered into their labours. And many of the Samaritans of that city believed on him for the saying of the woman, which testified, He told me all that ever I did. So when the Samaritans were come unto him, they besought him that he would tarry with them: and he abode there two days. And many more believed because of his own word; And said unto the woman, Now we believe, not because of thy saying: for we have heard him ourselves, and know that this is indeed the Christ, the Saviour of the world.

– John 4:34–42

1771. When you know you are a person of ideas that have appreciating value, be sure to know and be careful of the people you hook up with when you are on the ground floor, because many times the relationships could lead to manipulation. As you go up during the process, choose your friends wisely.

He that walketh with wise men shall be wise: but a companion of fools shall be destroyed.

– Proverbs 13:20

1772. Whether you are a high paid slave or a low paid slave, if you do not own the field, you're still a *slave*. Whether you're working in the field or working in the *big house*, if you're not an owner of the house or the field, you're still a slave!

Are you a slave? Don't let that bother you. But if you can win your freedom, you should. When the Lord chooses slaves, they become his free people. And when he chooses free people, they become slaves of Christ. God paid a great price for you. So don't become slaves of anyone else. Stay what you were when God chose you.

−1 Corinthians 7:21–24

Contemporary English Version (CEV)

And that ye study to be quiet, and to do your own business, and to work with your own hands, as we commanded you; That ye may walk honestly toward them that are without, and that ye may have lack of nothing.

−1 Thessalonians 4:11–12

1773. In some circles, a new idea will be celebrated and exalted as very valuable. It may be considered *priceless* or worth $1 million or more. In other circles, that same new idea will be passed by and counted as almost worthless. Determination of the value of a new idea is usually determined by the size of the minds of the circle of people that it's introduced to. Therefore, it's critical to choose the right circles when introducing a new idea.

A gift is as a precious stone in the eyes of him that hath it: whithersoever it turneth, it prospereth.

– Proverbs 17:8

A man's gift maketh room for him, and bringeth him before great men.

– Proverbs 18:16

1774. Every good man needs a good woman with *fire in her engine*, softness on her face, love in her heart, and intelligence in her brain, and to make her his wife.

Nevertheless, to avoid fornication, let every man have his own wife, and let every woman have her own husband.

–1 Corinthians 7:2

And the Lord God caused a deep sleep to fall upon Adam, and he slept: and he took one of his ribs, and closed up the flesh instead thereof; And the rib, which the Lord God had taken from man, made he a woman, and brought her unto the man. And Adam said, This is now bone of my bones, and flesh of my flesh: she shall be called Woman, because she was taken out of Man. Therefore shall a man leave his father and his mother, and shall cleave unto his wife: and they shall be one flesh. And they were both naked, the man and his wife, and were not ashamed.

– Genesis 2:21–25

Whoso findeth a wife findeth a good thing, and obtaineth favour of the Lord.

– Proverbs 18:22

1775. Take precautions, and thus, save repairs.

A prudent man foreseeth the evil, and hideth himself; but the simple pass on, and are punished.

– Proverbs 27:12

1776. The only way to heal the other person is to heal you. Never hate another. Rather, love yourself. Thus, freeing you from the hatred or manipulation of another person.

Ye have heard that it hath been said, Thou shalt love thy neighbour, and hate thine enemy. But I say unto you, Love your enemies, bless them that curse you, do good to them that hate you, and pray for them which despitefully use you, and persecute you; That ye may be the children of your Father which is in heaven: for he maketh his sun to rise on the evil and on the good, and sendeth rain on the just and on the unjust. For if ye love them which love you, what reward have ye? do not even the publicans the same? And if ye salute your brethren only, what do ye more than others? do not even the publicans so? Be ye therefore perfect, even as your Father which is in heaven is perfect.

– Matthew 5:43–48

Be not overcome of evil, but overcome evil with good.

– Romans 12:21

1777. I believe in the Bible, and the Bible has done me good!

And Jesus answered him, saying, It is written, That man shall not live by bread alone, but by every word of God.

– Luke 4:4

1778. You should seek the blessing that God promises to every person that worships and reverences Him. That is, to profit from the labor of your own hands, to be happy in life, to have a successful, fruitful family life, to live a long, healthy life, to see your children's children, and to see prosperity in your family from generation to generation. This is the promise and blessing of the Lord that you should pursue. It takes effort, but you should pursue it. You can accomplish it.

Blessed is every one that feareth the Lord; that walketh in his ways. For thou shalt eat the labour of thine hands: happy shalt thou be, and it shall be well with thee. Thy wife shall be as a fruitful vine by the sides of thine house: thy children like olive plants round about thy table. Behold, that thus shall the man be blessed that feareth the Lord. The Lord shall bless thee out of Zion: and thou shalt see the good of Jerusalem all the days of thy life. Yea, thou shalt see thy children's children, and peace upon Israel.

– Psalm 128

1779. God's grace can help you deal with the *real,* and cause your life to go from being less than ideal to becoming fulfilled.

Moreover the law entered, that the offence might abound. But where sin abounded, grace did much more abound.

– Romans 5:20

1780. Love is unfeigned commitment for an indefinite period of time. The commitment involves kindness, care, and the intentional betterment of the other person. There are no ulterior motives in addition to the choice and commitment to love.

Seeing ye have purified your souls in obeying the truth through the Spirit unto unfeigned love of the brethren, see that ye love one another with a pure heart fervently.

–1 Peter 1:22

1781. Recognition and acknowledgment of the truth regarding yourself and another will set you free from being manipulated by a facade. Awareness and transparency are empowering and liberating.

But speaking the truth in love, may grow up into him in all things, which is the head, *even* Christ.

– Ephesians 4:15

Open rebuke is better than secret love. Faithful are the wounds of a friend; but the kisses of an enemy are deceitful.

– Proverbs 27:5–6

1782. Thought has no color. Take time to gain superior thought, no matter where it comes from. Superior thought can come in various colors, and from various sources. Take time to get wisdom.

Buy the truth, and sell it not; also wisdom, and instruction, and understanding.

– Proverbs 23:23

1783. Regarding progress, you don't need the approval of people who are not doing anything in life. Neither do you need the approval of those who are doing nothing to help you go forward. *Go forward*! Your obligation is to God. Your assignment is to finish what God has given you to do. Take advantage of every profitable opportunity, and use the gifts and talents that God has given you.

Wherefore I perceive that there is nothing better, than that a man should rejoice in his own works; for that is his portion: for who shall bring him to see what shall be after him?

– Ecclesiastes 3:22

1784. Hold your peace, and don't let anyone steal it. Overcome evil with good. Overcome disorder with order. Overcome intimidation with calm confidence. Overcome blame with righteousness. Hold your peace, and don't let anyone steal it.

In your patience possess ye your souls.

– Luke 21:19

And Jesus stood before the governor: and the governor asked him, saying, Art thou the King of the Jews? And Jesus said unto him, Thou sayest. And when he was accused of the chief priests and elders, he answered nothing. Then said Pilate unto him, Hearest thou not how many things they witness against thee? And he answered him to never a word; insomuch that the governor marvelled greatly.

– Matthew 27:11–14

1785. If you ask anybody that is *somebody* how they became somebody, they will tell you that it took a lot of hard, smart work.

Seest thou a man diligent in his business? he shall stand before kings; he shall not stand before mean men.

– Proverbs 22:29

1786. Do not be disturbed by disturbing happenings in the news. God is stable. Even in uncertain times. God is committed to your future. There's a whole lot of more track on the *runway* of life! Be encouraged.

And ye shall hear of wars and rumours of wars: see that ye be not troubled: for all these things must come to pass, but the end is not yet.

– Matthew 24:6

1787. Once you make up your mind to actually *blast off* in life, life itself will begin to throw gas on you to escalate your acceleration. Blast off! There is nothing hindering you!

I can do all things through Christ, which strengtheneth me.

– Philippians 4:13

1788. What gets measured can be managed. Whether it's time, money, calories, steps, etc. What gets measured can be managed.

So teach us to number our days, that we may apply our hearts unto wisdom.

– Psalm 90:12

1789. Life can be eventful. Handle it with prayer.

And he spake a parable unto them *to this end*, that men ought always to pray, and not to faint.

– Luke 18:1

1790. God always responds to faith. Prosperity always responds to order. You need faith and order to create and maintain prosperity.

Let all things be done decently and in order.

–1 Corinthians 14:40

1791. Whatever you're facing in this moment, God has grace for you. Grace is God's ability to do for you, in you, or through you, what you don't have the ability to do in your own natural strength. It is God's *super* on your *natural*. God's grace will cause you to gain a supernatural result! Take time to worship, pray, and meditate on God's Word, the Bible. That's how you receive more of God's grace!

For if because of one man's trespass (lapse, offense) death reigned through that one, much more surely will those who receive [God's] overflowing grace (unmerited favor) and the free gift of righteousness [putting them into right standing with Himself] reign as kings in life through the one Man Jesus Christ (the Messiah, the Anointed One).

> – Romans 5:17
> Amplified Bible, Classic Edition (AMPC)

1792. The first stage of profit is *learning*.

Buy the truth, and sell it not; also wisdom, and instruction, and understanding.

> – Proverbs 23:23

1793. The longer you wait the less gets accomplished. You've got to stay on the run, to get the job done.

> –Pastor Avis Turner, MD

For a dream cometh through the multitude of business; and a fools voice is known by multitude of words.

> – Ecclesiastes 5:3

In the morning sow thy seed, and in the evening withhold not thine hand: for thou knowest not whether shall prosper, either this or that, or whether they both shall be alike good.

– Ecclesiastes 11:6

1794. Singing praise and worship music releases *endorphins* and *angels* on your behalf. Take time to sing praise and worship. You will be blessed and protected.

A merry heart maketh a cheerful countenance: but by sorrow of the heart the spirit is broken.

– Proverbs 15:13

The angel of the Lord encampeth round about them that fear him, and delivereth them. O taste and see that the Lord is good: blessed is the man that trusteth in him. O fear the Lord, ye his saints: for there is no want to them that fear him. The young lions do lack, and suffer hunger: but they that seek the Lord shall not want any good thing.

– Psalm 34:7–10

1795. There's rarely any drawback to keeping your mouth shut.

Even a fool, when he holdeth his peace, is counted wise: and he that shutteth his lips is esteemed a man of understanding.

– Proverbs 17:28

1796. A lot of times you can get more answers by being quiet than you can by talking.

Wherefore, my beloved brethren, let every man be swift to hear, slow to speak, slow to wrath.

– James 1:19

1797. Life is short. You've got to be patient.

The steps of a good man are ordered by the Lord: and he delighteth in his way.

– Psalm 37:23

1798. Life goes on. You should too!

Brethren, I count not myself to have apprehended: but this one thing I do, forgetting those things which are behind, and reaching forth unto those things which are before, I press toward the mark for the prize of the high calling of God in Christ Jesus.

– Philippians 3:13–14

1799. Never get so sophisticated that you can't say, "Thank You Jesus!"

In every thing give thanks: for this is the will of God in Christ Jesus concerning you.

−1 Thessalonians 5:18

1800. Life happens. You must be able to *pivot*.

I know both how to be abased, and I know how to abound: every where and in all things I am instructed both to be full and to be hungry, both to abound and to suffer need. I can do all things through Christ which strengtheneth me.

– Philippians 4:12–13

1801. Prior to every meeting, always remember that every conversation was *proceeded* by a conversation. Therefore, never be careless in your conversations.

The simple believeth every word: but the prudent man looketh well to his going.

– Proverbs 14:15

1802. When you have a destiny to accomplish, God is working harder than you are to make sure it comes to pass. However, you still have to work with God.

But Jesus answered them, My Father worketh hitherto, and I work.

– John 5:17

1803. We should never count people out based on their starting place. None of our families started out completely financially free. Those who have been able to struggle their way up should not condemn or discount those who are still in the struggle. If God did it for one person or family, He can do it for another. Temporary times, do not determine permanent destiny.

For the eyes of the Lord run to and fro throughout the whole earth, to shew himself strong in the behalf of them whose heart is perfect toward him...

–2 Chronicles 16:9a

1804. There's more than one way of teaching. If you're a good student, then you are able to adjust your learning capacity to the specific lessons of life.

The ear that heareth the reproof of life abideth among the wise.

– Proverbs 15:31

1805. Have a plan, yet, be open to the possibilities of God.

A man's heart deviseth his way: but the Lord directeth his steps.

– Proverbs 16:9

1806. Keep on producing with excellence. Make your *own* name. You won't need anyone else's name.

Yea, so have I strived to preach the gospel, not where Christ was named, lest I should build upon another man's foundation.

– Romans 15:20

1807. When people can *make* you, then, people can *break* you. Therefore, keep your eyes upon Jesus. Do what God has called you to do. Pay the price to become qualified. Then, make your *own* luck. If the *"powers that be"* seek to hold back an opportunity for you to play in their field, then find or build another field. When you're qualified to play, just play and win your own game.

And whatsoever ye do, do it heartily, as to the Lord, and not unto men; knowing that of the Lord ye shall receive the reward of the inheritance: for ye serve the Lord Christ.

– Colossians 3:23–24

1808. When you know your own value, you won't *cheapen* your asking price.

It is naught, it is naught, saith the buyer: but when he is gone his way, then he boasteth.

– Proverbs 20:14

1809. Don't spend your time tending to someone else's business. Rather, spend your time tending to your own business, because, that's what's going to *pay you*.

94

And that ye study to be quiet, and to do your own business, and to work with your own hands, as we commanded you; that ye may walk honestly toward them that are without, and that ye may have lack of nothing.

                    —1 Thessalonians 4:11–12

1810. Regarding creating a future for your family, go ahead! Go ahead! Somebody has to go ahead in order to create a prosperous posterity for your family. Don't be afraid to be the first. Don't be afraid to go ahead! Go ahead! Create a future for your family.

Now therefore be not grieved, nor angry with yourselves, that ye sold me hither: for God did send me before you to preserve life. For these two years hath the famine been in the land: and yet there are five years, in the which there shall neither be earing nor harvest. And God sent me before you to preserve you a posterity in the earth, and to save your lives by a great deliverance. So now it was not you that sent me hither, but God: and he hath made me a father to Pharaoh, and lord of all his house, and a ruler throughout all the land of Egypt. Haste ye, and go up to my father, and say unto him, Thus saith thy son Joseph, God hath made me lord of all Egypt: come down unto me, tarry not: and thou shalt dwell in the land of Goshen, and thou shalt be near unto me, thou, and thy children, and thy children's children, and thy flocks, and thy herds, and all that thou hast: and there will I nourish thee; for yet there are five years of famine; lest thou, and thy household, and all that thou hast, come to poverty.

– Genesis 45:5–11

1811. We are saved by grace, through faith, and not by works, lest anyone should boast. Therefore, if you're saved by grace, and do not do any good works, you can still be saved. However, you won't be satisfied. Satisfaction comes from accomplishing great deeds, whether large or small. Salvation is by grace, through faith. Satisfaction is by accomplishing what God created you to do.

For we are his workmanship, created in Christ Jesus unto good works, which God hath before ordained that we should walk in them.

– Ephesians 2:10

1812. God often takes the foolish things of the world to confound the wise, and all of us have been a little foolish at times. And some of us, whom we've considered wise, are often sometimes otherwise.

But God hath chosen the foolish things of the world to confound the wise; and God hath chosen the weak things of the world to confound the things which are mighty; and base things of the world, and things which are despised, hath God chosen, yea, and things which are not, to bring to nought things that are: that no flesh should glory in his presence. But of him are ye in Christ Jesus, who of God is made unto us wisdom, and righteousness, and sanctification, and redemption: that, according as it is written, He that glorieth, let him glory in the Lord.

–1 Corinthians 1:27–31

1813. Just do the right thing, and don't decide what you are going to do based on popular opinion. You'll be happier in the end!

Blessed is the man that walketh not in the counsel of the ungodly, nor standeth in the way of sinners, nor sitteth in the seat of the scornful. But his delight is in the law of the Lord; and in his law doth he meditate day and night. And he shall be like a tree planted by the rivers of water, that bringeth forth his fruit in his season; his leaf also shall not wither; and whatsoever he doeth shall prosper.

– Psalm 1:1–3

1814. You can't hide quality, and you can't really fake it. You must develop it. Be the best at what God made you to do, and be the best you that God made you to be, by continual self–development.

Seest thou a man diligent in his business? he shall stand before kings; he shall not stand before mean men.

– Proverbs 22:29

1815. People who are not doing anything have nothing better to do than to talk about people who are doing something. Therefore, the best thing for people who are doing something to do is to ignore the talk of those who are not doing anything. Those who are doing something don't have time to talk about others.

He that is despised, and hath a servant, is better than he that honoureth himself, and lacketh bread.

— Proverbs 12:9

1816. If Christians would pray several times a day, we would be less carnal, more spiritual, and more successful. As we stay in continual fellowship with Jehovah, the God of the universe, we will act, talk, and look more like Him.

Seven times a day do I praise thee because of thy righteous judgments. Great peace have they which love thy law: and nothing shall offend them.

— Psalm 119:164–165

1817. God sometimes sends us signs in our times of need to let us know He's with us and that His promises are sure. Take time to meditate God's Word, the Bible, for faith comes by hearing and hearing by the Word of God. We are the just. We live by our faith, not by signs. However, it's always special when God increases our joy with beautiful signs of His faithfulness and favor!

Shew me a token for good; that they which hate me may see it, and be ashamed: because thou, Lord, hast holpen me, and comforted me.

— Psalm 86:17

1818. When you know your ways please the Lord, you can have soul satisfaction! You know you're doing alright. Nothing else besides has very much consequence. You please the Lord by obeying His principles in the Bible. Study, learn, meditate, listen to, and practice God's principles. The promised rewards will be forthcoming!

When a man's ways please the Lord, he maketh even his enemies to be at peace with him.

– Proverbs 16:7

1819. If we will restrict our diets while we are free to choose, we won't be forced to restrict our diets.

All things are lawful unto me, but all things are not expedient: all things are lawful for me, but I will not be brought under the power of any.

–1 Corinthians 6:12

Know ye not that they which run in a race run all, but one receiveth the prize? So run, that ye may obtain. And every man that striveth for the mastery is temperate in all things. Now they do it to obtain a corruptible crown; but we an incorruptible. I therefore so run, not as uncertainly; so fight I, not as one that beateth the air: But I keep under my body, and bring it into subjection: lest that by any means, when I have preached to others, I myself should be a castaway.

–1 Corinthians 9:24–27

1820. We often miss potential miracles, because we fail to notice and value the flowers that grow in between the cracks of time. Every miracle may not happen on your schedule. However, you must be alert enough to capture the potential beauty when it arises. Capture that good idea, story, song, solution, relationship, conversation, etc. These are miraculous flowers that grow in between the cracks.

I am the rose of Sharon, and the lily of the valleys.

– Song of Solomon 2:1

1821. In life, you have to *take* opportunities! They're not just handed to you. You must take opportunities for rest, recreation, idea creation, advancement, etc. You must take opportunities, because, in most cases, they will not just be handed to you.

And he said unto them, Come ye yourselves apart into a desert place, and rest a while: for there were many coming and going, and they had no leisure so much as to eat.

– Mark 6:31

1822. In regard to the will of God, if you haven't succeeded, it's because you haven't done your best. If you do your best, you'll be a success. Either, there's a lack of knowledge or a lack of *action* upon the knowledge that you have. However, when you act upon the knowledge of God, you will succeed. So, if you haven't succeeded, it's because you haven't done your best. You were made in the image and likeness of God! You were born to succeed!

I have said, Ye are gods; and all of you are children of the most High.

– Psalm 82:6

And God said, Let us make man in our image, after our likeness: and let them have dominion over the fish of the sea, and over the fowl of the air, and over the cattle, and over all the earth, and over every creeping thing that creepeth upon the earth. So God created man in his own image, in the image of God created he him; male and female created he them. And God blessed them, and God said unto them, Be fruitful, and multiply, and replenish the earth, and subdue it: and have dominion over the fish of the sea, and over the fowl of the air, and over every living thing that moveth upon the earth.

– Genesis 1:26–28

1823. Don't settle for defeat! Keep striving to do your best, in spite of setbacks or opposition! There's more in you than you know! Don't settle for defeat! Keep striving for the best! Stay in the race!

Fight the good fight of faith, lay hold on eternal life, whereunto thou art also called, and hast professed a good profession before many witnesses.

–1 Timothy 6:12

1824. Challenges make champions better!

Know ye not that they which run in a race run all, but one receiveth the prize? So run, that ye may obtain. And every man that striveth for the mastery is temperate in all things. Now they do it to obtain a corruptible crown; but we an incorruptible. I therefore so run, not as uncertainly; so fight I, not as one that beateth the air: But I keep under my body, and bring it into subjection: lest that by any means, when I have preached to others, I myself should be a castaway.

–1 Corinthians 9:24–27

1825. God doesn't bring His Word down to our performance. He brings His grace down to our performance, in order to help us come up to the standards of His Word. However, He never lowers the standard of His Word. He exalts His Word above His name. All things are upheld by His Word. However, we are upheld by His grace.

For the word of God is quick, and powerful, and sharper than any twoedged sword, piercing even to the dividing asunder of soul and spirit, and of the joints and marrow, and is a discerner of the thoughts and intents of the heart. Neither is there any creature that is not manifest in his sight: but all things are naked and opened unto the eyes of him with whom we have to do. Seeing then that we have a great high priest, that is passed into the heavens, Jesus the Son of God, let us hold fast our profession. For we have not an high priest which cannot be touched with the feeling of our infirmities; but was in all points tempted like as we are, yet without sin. Let us therefore come boldly unto the throne of grace, that we may obtain mercy, and find grace to help in time of need.

– Hebrews 4:12–16

1826. Regarding success, it's about execution. And, it's not over until the *cash register sings!*

In all labour there is profit: but the talk of the lips tendeth only to penury.

– Proverbs 14:23

1827. Be the CEO of your *own* life. Set your own goals. Set your own deadlines. Then, do what's necessary to accomplish them. Be accountable to yourself, and keep your own counsel. Be your own boss.

Wherefore I perceive that there is nothing better, than that a man should rejoice in his own works; for that is his portion: for who shall bring him to see what shall be after him?

– Ecclesiastes 3:22

1828. Jump–start your day with a song of praise! Recognize God as the "Author" of your new day! Give Him thanksgiving for blessing you in all your ways. Jump–start each day with a song of praise! God deserves it, and you will feel better. Don't leave any room for complaining at the beginning of the day. Jump-start the morning with simple, sincere praise. You are inviting God's comfort and wisdom into your day!

It is a good thing to give thanks unto the Lord, and to sing praises unto thy name, O Most High: To shew forth thy lovingkindness in the morning, and thy faithfulness every night.

– Psalm 92:1–2

1829. Don't be a slave, no matter what color your procuring master may be! Always maintain your liberty as a self–sufficient person, made in the image and likeness of God Almighty!

Are you a slave? Don't let that bother you. But if you can win your freedom, you should. When the Lord chooses slaves, they become his free people. And when he chooses free people, they become slaves of Christ. God paid a great price for you. So don't become slaves of anyone else. Stay what you were when God chose you.

–1 Corinthians 7:21–24

Contemporary English Version (CEV)

1830. You should live in such a way that you get *good mail* everyday!

As cold waters to a thirsty soul, so is good news from a far country.

– Proverbs 25:25

1831. May you serve and care for your customers, employees, and subordinates according to the integrity, love, and care of your heart, and manage them according to the skillfulness, discernment, sobriety, and discretion of your mind. It takes a careful combination of qualities of heart and mind to be a great leader.

He chose David also his servant, and took him from the sheepfolds: From following the ewes great with young he brought him to feed Jacob his people, and Israel his inheritance. So he fed them according to the integrity of his heart; and guided them by the skilfulness of his hands.

– Psalm 78:70–72

1832. Learn a lesson from the birds: talk to and praise God early in the morning.

It is a good thing to give thanks unto the Lord, and to sing praises unto thy name, O Most High: To shew forth thy lovingkindness in the morning, and thy faithfulness every night.

– Psalm 92:1–2

And in the morning, rising up a great while before day, he went out, and departed into a solitary place, and there prayed.

– Mark 1:35

1833. Regarding business, *crooks* like creeks eventually dry up.

A false balance is abomination to the Lord: but a just weight is his delight.

– Proverbs 11:1

1834. Most people are full of excuses today, and full of *regrets* tomorrow. Take action today, and you'll be happier tomorrow.

Whatsoever thy hand findeth to do, do it with thy might; for there is no work, nor device, nor knowledge, nor wisdom, in the grave, whither thou goest. I returned, and saw under the sun, that the race is not to the swift, nor the battle to the strong, neither yet bread to the wise, nor yet riches to men of understanding, nor yet favour to men of skill; but time and chance happeneth to them all.

– Ecclesiastes 9:10–11

1835. You're smart! In regard to doing something, don't be afraid to keep your own counsel, because nothing was ever the right way of doing something, until someone successfully did it, and then it became the right way. Then, someone else copied what that person did. So, don't be afraid to keep your own counsel. You're smart! Go right ahead!

But let every man prove his own work, and then shall he have rejoicing in himself alone, and not in another.

– Galatians 6:4

1836. Don't be afraid to be uncommon, and to acknowledge the fact that you are uncommon, because only through your acknowledgement of the fact that you are uncommon, will you be able to offer and give properly your uncommon gift to the world.

Jesus answered and said unto her, If thou knewest the gift of God, and who it is that saith to thee, Give me to drink; thou wouldest have asked of him, and he would have given thee living water.

– John 4:10

That the communication of thy faith may become effectual by the acknowledging of every good thing which is in you in Christ Jesus.

– Philemon 6:1

1837. When you submit your will to God's will, there's nothing in Earth, Heaven, or in Hell that can withstand the force of that *will*, because when you submit to God's will, it shall come to pass. You can do all things through Christ, which strengthens you, and if God be for you, who can be against you?

What shall we then say to these things? If God be for us, who can be against us?

– Romans 8:31

1838. Never replace the *brand* of God, for the brand of man. God brands your heart. Man attempts to brand your mind. Take time to renew your mind with the Word of God, and thereby, *brand* your life.

I beseech you therefore, brethren, by the mercies of God, that ye present your bodies a living sacrifice, holy, acceptable unto God, which is your reasonable service. And be not conformed to this world: but be ye transformed by the renewing of your mind, that ye may prove what is that good, and acceptable, and perfect, will of God.

– Romans 12:1–2

1839. Wisdom would've made Jesus cut Judas off immediately when He realized that he was stealing. However, Jesus committed to Judas, even unto the death of the cross. At the Last Supper, John, the beloved, was on one side, but Judas was on the other side. Jesus committed to loving him, even unto the end, because grace bridges the gap between wisdom and love. Love commits to the end. Love never fails.

When Jesus had thus said, he was troubled in spirit, and testified, and said, Verily, verily, I say unto you, that one of you shall betray me. Then the disciples looked one on another, doubting of whom he spake. Now there was leaning on Jesus bosom one of his disciples, whom Jesus loved. Simon Peter therefore beckoned to him, that he should ask who it should be of whom he spake. He then lying on Jesus breast saith unto him, Lord, who is it? Jesus answered, He it is, to whom I shall give a sop, when I have dipped it. And when he had dipped the sop, he gave it to Judas Iscariot, the son of Simon. And after the sop Satan entered into him. Then said Jesus unto him, That thou doest, do quickly. Now no man at the table knew for what intent he spake this unto him. For some of them thought, because Judas had the bag, that Jesus had said unto him, Buy those things that we have need of against the feast; or, that he should give something to the poor. He then having received the sop went immediately out: and it was night. Therefore, when he was gone out, Jesus said, Now is the Son of man glorified, and God is glorified in him.

– John 13:21–31

1840. Love can be painful sometimes. That's why it's called *long-suffering*. Sometimes, that truth feels better known, than practiced. Yet, it is the true heart of God.

Charity suffereth long, and is kind...

–1 Corinthians 13:4a

Put on therefore, as the elect of God, holy and beloved, bowels of mercies, kindness, humbleness of mind, meekness, longsuffering; forbearing one another, and forgiving one another, if any man have a quarrel against any: even as Christ forgave you, so also do ye. And above all these things put on charity, which is the bond of perfectness. And let the peace of God rule in your hearts, to the which also ye are called in one body; and be ye thankful. Let the word of Christ dwell in you richly in all wisdom; teaching and admonishing one another in psalms and hymns and spiritual songs, singing with grace in your hearts to the Lord. And whatsoever ye do in word or deed, do all in the name of the Lord Jesus, giving thanks to God and the Father by him.

– Colossians 3:12–17

1841. Grace bridges the gap between wisdom and love, and it thus, becomes true wisdom, which is godly wisdom, because God is love.

Who is a wise man and endued with knowledge among you? let him shew out of a good conversation his works with meekness of wisdom. But if ye have bitter envying and strife in your hearts, glory not, and lie not against the truth. This wisdom descendeth not from above, but is earthly, sensual, devilish. For where envying and strife is, there is confusion and every evil work. But the wisdom that is from above is first pure, then peaceable, gentle, and easy to be intreated, full of mercy and good fruits, without partiality, and without hypocrisy. And the fruit of righteousness is sown in peace of them that make peace.

– James 3:13–18

1842. True love doesn't require you to let yourself be abused. That would not be true love. True love begins with you loving *you*!

Jesus said unto him, Thou shalt love the Lord thy God with all thy heart, and with all thy soul, and with all thy mind. This is the first and great commandment. And the second is like unto it, Thou shalt love thy neighbour as thyself. On these two commandments hang all the law and the prophets.

– Matthew 22:37–40

1843. Even great people make excuses to mark history in their favor. Greater people take responsibility, and let history decide the tale.

Most men will proclaim every one his own goodness: but a faithful man who can find?

– Proverbs 20:6

Great men are not always wise: neither do the aged understand judgment.

– Job 32:9

1844. Parenting is not about perfection. Parenting is about doing enough of the right things that your children will have a path to follow when they become adults, because they've seen enough of the right things in your life when they were children, that they can live their life by what they've learned from you when they become adults.

Train up a child in the way he should go: and when he is old, he will not depart from it.

– Proverbs 22:6

And the Lord said, Shall I hide from Abraham that thing which I do; Seeing that Abraham shall surely become a great and mighty nation, and all the nations of the earth shall be blessed in him? For I know him, that he will command his children and his household after him, and they shall keep the way of the Lord, to do justice and judgment; that the Lord may bring upon Abraham that which he hath spoken of him.

– Genesis 18:17–19

1845. God will "turn back time" for you to get the miracle He has promised you. Just position yourself through obedience to His principles, and you can still obtain your destiny.

And Isaiah said, This sign shalt thou have of the Lord, that the Lord will do the thing that he hath spoken: shall the shadow go forward ten degrees, or go back ten degrees? And Hezekiah answered, It is a light thing for the shadow to go down ten degrees: nay, but let the shadow return backward ten degrees. And Isaiah the prophet cried unto the Lord: and he brought the shadow ten degrees backward, by which it had gone down in the dial of Ahaz.

–2 Kings 20:9–11

And I will restore to you the years that the locust hath eaten, the cankerworm, and the caterpiller, and the palmerworm, my great army which I sent among you. And ye shall eat in plenty, and be satisfied, and praise the name of the Lord your God, that hath dealt wondrously with you: and my people shall never be ashamed.

– Joel 2:25–26

1846. When you truly commit to accomplishing God's will for your life, and you're willing to fight for it, no matter what, God will stop the clock for you! In fact, He will *turn back time* in order to help you finish what He already predetermined for you to finish. All He needs is your commitment. If you're willing to "fight the good fight of faith" you will win, no matter what!

Then spake Joshua to the Lord in the day when
the Lord delivered up the Amorites before the children of Israel, and he said in the sight of Israel, Sun, stand thou still upon Gibeon; and thou, Moon, in the valley of Ajalon. And the sun stood still, and the moon stayed, until the people had avenged themselves upon their enemies. Is not this written in the book of Jasher? So the sun stood still in the midst of heaven, and hasted not to go down about a whole day. And there was no day like that before it or after it, that
the Lord hearkened unto the voice of a man: for
the Lord fought for Israel.

– Joshua 10:12–14

1847. Start the day with praise and worship, and you'll start the day as an unequivocal victor and success! There's nothing that can withstand the force of sincere praise and worship!

It is a good thing to give thanks unto the Lord, and to sing praises unto thy name, O Most High: To shew forth thy

lovingkindness in the morning, and thy faithfulness every night.

– Psalm 92:1–2

1848. Without action there's no satisfaction. Without action there are no results. Without action there's no fulfillment of the promise!

But whoso looketh into the perfect law of liberty, and continueth therein, he being not a forgetful hearer, but a doer of the work, this man shall be blessed in his deed.

– James 1:25

1849. If it seems like your blessing has been "a-long-time-coming", then what God is doing is allowing you to "walk-it-out", so that when you finish obtaining that blessing, you will know what you're talking about, and no one, nowhere, at anytime, will be able to deny you the wisdom that you have learned from walking out your blessing. You can then teach it and help someone else after you.

But whoso looketh into the perfect law of liberty, and continueth therein, he being not a forgetful hearer, but a doer of the work, this man shall be blessed in his deed.

– James 1:25

1850. Be your own cheerleader! Only you are responsible to know exactly what it takes to motivate you. Don't put that responsibility on anyone else. Otherwise, you may be disappointed, and they may be apathetic or clueless of your expectation. Be your own cheerleader. You will be more consistently motivated.

Wherefore I perceive that there is nothing better, than that a man should rejoice in his own works; for that is his portion: for who shall bring him to see what shall be after him?

– Ecclesiastes 3:22

1851. Success takes what it takes. Don't be afraid or discouraged by the time that it takes to succeed. You don't have anything else to do, but fail, if you don't go for it! So, *go for it*! Success will be "right–on–time" if you simply go for it!

What profit hath he that worketh in that wherein he laboureth? I have seen the travail, which God hath given to the sons of men to be exercised in it. He hath made every thing beautiful in his time: also he hath set the world in their heart, so that no man can find out the work that God maketh from the beginning to the end. I know that there is no good in them, but for a man to rejoice, and to do good in his life. And also that every man should eat and drink, and enjoy the good of all his labour, it is the gift of God.

– Ecclesiastes 3:9–13

1852. The common practice of writing books has no end. The uncommon practice of reading books rarely has a beginning. Those who pursue the uncommon practice of reading books have more aptitude toward writing books. They also have greater results from the content gained within the pages. Thus, their very lives become positive lessons that can fill the pages of new books.

And moreover, because the preacher was wise, he still taught the people knowledge; yea, he gave good heed, and sought out, and set in order many proverbs. The preacher sought to find out acceptable words: and that which was written was upright, even words of truth. The words of the wise are as goads, and as nails fastened by the masters of assemblies, which are given from one shepherd. And further, by these, my son, be admonished: of making many books there is no end; and much study is a weariness of the flesh. Let us hear the conclusion of the whole matter: Fear God, and keep his commandments: for this is the whole duty of man. For God shall bring every work into judgment, with every secret thing, whether it be good, or whether it be evil.

– Ecclesiastes 12:9–14

1853. Some Christians demonstrate certain habits and behavior that leave you puzzled and asking them, "Are you saved?"

Abstain from all appearance of evil.

–1 Thessalonians 5:22

1854. Success is not overnight. However, success is *every* night. To achieve and maintain success takes every day and every night.

In the morning sow thy seed, and in the evening withhold not thine hand: for thou knowest not whether shall prosper, either this or that, or whether they both shall be alike good.

– Ecclesiastes 11:6

1855. Pay off your small credit cards as soon as possible, because the *"small foxes"* spoil the credit!

Take us the foxes, the little foxes, that spoil the vines: for our vines have tender grapes.

– Song of Solomon 2:15

The rich ruleth over the poor, and the borrower is servant to the lender.

– Proverbs 22:7

Owe no man any thing, but to love one another: for he that loveth another hath fulfilled the law.

– Romans 13:8

1856. If you want to get out of the *"hood"*, then, you need to take times away from the 'hood. Take your children on trips to see things outside of your normal neighborhood. Get out of your normal environment. If you want to be more, you need to *see* more. If you want to get out of the 'hood, then, get away from the 'hood!

Now the Lord had said unto Abram, Get thee out of thy country, and from thy kindred, and from thy fathers house, unto a land that I will shew thee: And I will make of thee a great nation, and I will bless thee, and make thy name great; and thou shalt be a blessing: And I will bless them that bless thee, and curse him that curseth thee: and in thee shall all families of the earth be blessed. So Abram departed, as the Lord had spoken unto him; and Lot went with him: and Abram was seventy and five years old when he departed out of Haran. And Abram took Sarai his wife, and Lot his brother's son, and all their substance that they had gathered, and the souls that they had gotten in Haran; and they went forth to go into the land of Canaan; and into the land of Canaan they came.

– Genesis 12:1–5

1857. The only thing that determines whether something is one person's junk or another person's treasure is the degree of thankfulness or the lack thereof.

The full soul loatheth an honeycomb; but to the hungry soul every bitter thing is sweet.

– Proverbs 27:7

1858. Faithfulness in living, giving, and loving is the key to long–term success for you and your family. It is a controllable key for obtaining blessing in your generation and passing down blessings to future generations. Be faithful in living, giving, and loving. It is the key to long-term success.

When I call to remembrance the unfeigned faith that is in thee, which dwelt first in thy grandmother Lois, and thy mother Eunice; and I am persuaded that in thee also. Wherefore I put thee in remembrance that thou stir up the gift of God, which is in thee by the putting on of my hands.

–2 Timothy 1:5–6

1859. As a righteous person, you can be assured of the blessing of God upon you and all that you do today. His loving favor surrounds you like a shield. His eyes are upon the sparrow, and you know He watches over you. Be blessed and secure, and rest in His love today. In Jesus name, amen.

Are not two sparrows sold for a farthing? and one of them shall not fall on the ground without your Father. But the very hairs of your head are all numbered. Fear ye not therefore, ye are of more value than many sparrows.

– Matthew 10:29–31

1860. Whether in love or war, money and wisdom determines power. Wise is the person who discerns the potency and efficacy of the use of each.

Wisdom is good with an inheritance: and by it there is profit to them that see the sun. For wisdom is a defence, and money is a defence: but the excellency of knowledge is, that wisdom giveth life to them that have it.

– Ecclesiastes 7:11–12

1861. I know too much to be taken advantage of. I don't know enough to not be taken advantage of. I know enough to find out what I need to know to not be taken advantage of.

Also, that the soul be without knowledge, it is not good; and he that hasteth with his feet sinneth.

– Proverbs 19:2

1862. Critics are rarely producers. However, they seek to benefit from the value produced by others.

It is naught, it is naught, saith the buyer: but when he is gone his way, then he boasteth.

– Proverbs 20:14

1863. People who have extra *did extra.*

Then shall the kingdom of heaven be likened unto ten virgins, which took their lamps, and went forth to meet the bridegroom. And five of them were wise, and five were foolish. They that were foolish took their lamps, and took no oil with them: but the wise took oil in their vessels with their lamps. While the bridegroom tarried, they all slumbered and slept. And at midnight there was a cry made, Behold, the bridegroom cometh; go ye out to meet him. Then all those virgins arose, and trimmed their lamps. And the foolish said unto the wise, Give us of your oil; for our lamps are gone out. But the wise answered, saying, Not so; lest there be not enough for us and you: but go ye rather to them that sell, and buy for yourselves. And while they went to buy, the bridegroom came; and they that were ready went in with him to the marriage: and the door was shut. Afterward came also the other virgins, saying, Lord, Lord, open to us. But he answered and said, Verily I say unto you, I know you not. Watch therefore, for ye know neither the day nor the hour wherein the Son of man cometh.

– Matthew 25:1–13

1864. No one person or group of people has the monopoly on good ideas. The only person who has a monopoly on good ideas is the one who takes *action* on those ideas, because every time a new idea comes forth, it resets the standard of what is right, acceptable, and possible. Action is what truly determines who the "trend–setters" are. Take action on your ideas, because you are a *trend–setter*!

Even so faith, if it hath not works, is dead, being alone. Yea, a man may say, Thou hast faith, and I have works: shew me thy faith without thy works, and I will shew thee my faith by my works.

– James 2:17–18

1865. You can always tell if someone is threatened by the excellence of what you're doing, by listening to what they're saying. Are they spending their *airtime* talking about the benefits of what they're doing? Or, are they spending time fighting what you're doing? How they expend their energies will reveal the focus of their fight. It will either be against what threatens their influence or for the importance of their own mission.

Do we begin again to commend ourselves? or need we, as some others, epistles of commendation to you, or letters of commendation from you? Ye are our epistle written in our hearts, known and read of all men: Forasmuch as ye are manifestly declared to be the epistle of Christ ministered by us, written not with ink, but with the Spirit of the living God; not in tables of stone, but in fleshy tables of the heart.

–2 Corinthians 3:1–3

For we dare not make ourselves of the number, or compare ourselves with some that commend themselves: but they measuring themselves by themselves, and comparing themselves among themselves, are not wise.

–2 Corinthians 10:12

1866. Most people are shallow listeners, moved only by the rises and falls of emotions and words without capturing the true meaning. You need meaning in order to change your life. You have to be a discriminating listener in order to gain the truth. Truth is what sets you free. Jesus said, "If you continue in my doctrine, then are you my disciples indeed, and you shall know the truth, and the truth shall make you free."

Then said Jesus to those Jews which believed on him, If ye continue in my word, then are ye my disciples indeed; and ye shall know the truth, and the truth shall make you free.

– John 8:31–32

The sower soweth the word. And these are they by the way side, where the word is sown; but when they have heard, Satan cometh immediately, and taketh away the word that was sown in their hearts. And these are they likewise which are sown on stony ground; who, when they have heard the word, immediately receive it with gladness; and have no root in themselves, and so endure but for a time: afterward, when affliction or persecution ariseth for the words sake, immediately they are offended. And these are they which are sown among thorns; such as hear the word, and the cares of this world, and the deceitfulness of riches, and the lusts of other things entering in, choke the word, and it becometh unfruitful. And these are they which are sown on good ground; such as hear the word, and receive it, and bring forth fruit, some thirtyfold, some sixty, and some an hundred.

– Mark 4:14–20

1867. Some people love you just because. Some people love you *because*. Always know the difference, and know that true love is a free gift.

But God commendeth his love toward us, in that, while we were yet sinners, Christ died for us.

– Romans 5:8

1868. To the person who has ears to hear, let them hear: When you spend a couple of hours praying in the Holy Ghost, don't be concerned if you don't understand all of what you've prayed out. Just be confident in knowing that because you spent time talking to God, the answer will be forthcoming. And, the answer is *"all good!"*

For he that speaketh in an unknown tongue speaketh not unto men, but unto God: for no man understandeth him; howbeit in the spirit he speaketh mysteries.

–1 Corinthians 14:2

1869. After you've had a long day, the habit of meditating the Word of God will reconstitute you into a full, whole, strong man or woman.

I beseech you therefore, brethren, by the mercies of God, that ye present your bodies a living sacrifice, holy, acceptable unto God, which is your reasonable service. And be not conformed to this world: but be ye transformed by the renewing of your mind, that ye may prove what is that good, and acceptable, and perfect, will of God.

– Romans 12:1–2

1870. The Word of God will transform you!

I beseech you therefore, brethren, by the mercies of God, that ye present your bodies a living sacrifice, holy, acceptable unto God, which is your reasonable service. And be not conformed to this world: but be ye transformed by the renewing of your mind, that ye may prove what is that good, and acceptable, and perfect, will of God.

– Romans 12:1–2

1871. Do not be conformed to this world and its way of thinking. Rather, be a *transformer*! Transform your mind by the Word of God! Meditate God's Word daily. Read the Word! Speak the Word! Live out the Word! You will truly be a transformer! Your life will be changed, and you'll help to change others.

Ye are the salt of the earth: but if the salt have lost his savour, wherewith shall it be salted? it is thenceforth good for nothing, but to be cast out, and to be trodden under foot of men. Ye are the light of the world. A city that is set on an hill cannot be hid. Neither do men light a candle, and put it under a bushel, but on a candlestick; and it giveth light unto all that are in the house. Let your light so shine before men, that they may see your good works, and glorify your Father which is in heaven.

– Matthew 5:13–16

1872. You're blessed! O' so blessed today! The Lord is working on your behalf! It's good to be you today!

And it shall come to pass, if thou shalt hearken diligently unto the voice of the Lord thy God, to observe and to do all his commandments which I command thee this day, that the Lord thy God will set thee on high above all nations of the earth: And all these blessings shall come on thee, and overtake thee, if thou shalt hearken unto the voice of the Lord thy God. Blessed shalt thou be in the city, and blessed shalt thou be in the field. Blessed shall be the fruit of thy body, and the fruit of thy ground, and the fruit of thy cattle, the increase of thy kine, and the flocks of thy sheep. Blessed shall be thy basket and thy store. Blessed shalt thou be when thou comest in, and blessed shalt thou be when thou goest out. The Lord shall cause thine enemies that rise up against thee to be smitten before thy face: they shall come out against thee one way, and flee before thee seven ways. The Lord shall command the blessing upon thee in thy storehouses, and in all that thou settest thine hand unto; and he shall bless thee in the land which the Lord thy God giveth thee. The Lord shall establish thee an holy people unto himself, as he hath sworn unto thee, if thou shalt keep the commandments of the Lord thy God, and walk in his ways. And all people of the earth shall see that thou art called by the name of the Lord; and they shall be afraid of thee. And the Lord shall make thee plenteous in goods, in the fruit of thy body, and in the fruit of thy cattle, and in the fruit of thy ground, in the land which the Lord sware unto thy fathers to give thee. The Lord shall open unto thee his good treasure, the heaven to give the rain unto thy land in his season, and to bless all the work of thine hand: and thou shalt lend unto many nations, and thou shalt not borrow. And the Lord shall make thee the head, and not the tail; and thou shalt be above only, and thou shalt not be beneath; if that thou hearken unto the commandments of the Lord thy God, which I command thee this day, to observe and to do them: And thou shalt not go aside from any of the words which I command thee this day, to the right hand, or to the left, to go after other gods to serve them.

– Deuteronomy 28:1–14

1873. The reasons to praise the Lord just keep multiplying hour by hour; day by day; and year by year! Take time to count the many reasons to praise Him today! You will feel much better!

It is a good thing to give thanks unto the Lord, and to sing praises unto thy name, O Most High: To shew forth thy lovingkindness in the morning, and thy faithfulness every night.

– Psalm 92:1–2

1874. Don't get stuck in a *box*! If it *wins*, it's right! Success is found right outside of the box! Stretch your thinking. If it wins, it's right! Don't get stuck in a *box*!

And Jesus said unto them, Because of your unbelief: for verily I say unto you, If ye have faith as a grain of mustard seed, ye shall say unto this mountain, Remove hence to yonder place; and it shall remove; and nothing shall be impossible unto you. Howbeit this kind goeth not out but by prayer and fasting.

– Matthew 17:20–21

1875. As you feed upon God's Word, by actively, intentionally using it as a tool to advance in life, you will discover new levels of productivity.

What advantage then hath the Jew? or what profit is there of circumcision? Much every way: chiefly, because that unto them were committed the oracles of God. For what if some did not believe? shall their unbelief make the faith of God without effect? God forbid: yea, let God be true, but every man a liar; as it is written, That thou mightest be justified in thy sayings, and mightest overcome when thou art judged.

– Romans 3:1–4

1876. Truth offends or it invites. No one can ignore it, because it is the truth. Everyone seeks the truth. It either offends or it invites, but it cannot be ignored, because it is the truth.

For my flesh is meat indeed, and my blood is drink indeed. He that eateth my flesh, and drinketh my blood, dwelleth in me, and I in him. As the living Father hath sent me, and I live by the Father: so he that eateth me, even he shall live by me. This is that bread which came down from heaven: not as your fathers did eat manna, and are dead: he that eateth of this bread shall live for ever. These things said he in the synagogue, as he taught in Capernaum. Many therefore of his disciples, when they had heard this, said, This is an hard saying; who can hear it? When Jesus knew in himself that his disciples murmured at it, he said unto them, Doth this offend you? What and if ye shall see the Son of man ascend up where he was before? It is the spirit that quickeneth; the flesh profiteth nothing: the words that I speak unto you, they are spirit, and they are life. But there are some of you that believe not. For Jesus knew from the beginning who they were that believed not, and who should betray him. And he said, Therefore, said I unto you, that no man can come unto me, except it were given unto him of my Father. From that time many of his disciples went back, and walked no more with him. Then said Jesus unto the twelve, Will ye also go away? Then Simon Peter answered him, Lord, to whom shall we go? thou hast the words of eternal life.

– John 6:55–68

1877. It's all about Jesus. If you lose sight of that, then, you've lost the *whole ball of wax!*

Jesus saith unto him, I am the way, the truth, and the life: no man cometh unto the Father, but by me.

– John 14:6

Be it known unto you all, and to all the people of Israel, that by the name of Jesus Christ of Nazareth, whom ye crucified, whom God raised from the dead, *even* by him doth this man stand here before you whole. This is the stone which was set at nought of you builders, which is become the head of the corner. Neither is there salvation in any other: for there is none other name under heaven given among men, whereby we must be saved.

– Acts 4:10–12

1878. Read the Bible everyday. Pray everyday. Sing songs of worship to God everyday. There will be days when you will not clearly see your answer. However, because you have a habit of continual fellowship with God, He can lead you without you physically or tangibly realizing it. Your thoughts and actions will simply be the right ones. You will be integrally aligned with the mind of God Almighty. You are flesh of His flesh, and bone of His bones. You are one spirit with the Lord.

Wherefore, my beloved, as ye have always obeyed, not as in my presence only, but now much more in my absence, work out your own salvation with fear and trembling. For it is God which worketh in you both to will and to do of his good pleasure.

– Philippians 2:12–13

1879. Unreleased potential fails to benefit you.

In all labour there is profit: but the talk of the lips tendeth only to penury.

– Proverbs 14:23

1880. Life is a collection of moments. Whether in marriage, conversations, sports, school, college, watching the Olympics, enjoying meals, coffee, tea, etc. Life is a collection of moments. Savor the moments, and make the most of your life!

He hath made every thing beautiful in his time: also he hath set the world in their heart, so that no man can find out the work that God maketh from the beginning to the end.

– Ecclesiastes 3:11

1881. If you're patient enough, and you give yourself enough learning time, you can eliminate *begging*. Begging is a result of lack. It's a result of lack of knowledge, lack of resources, lack of "*know how*", and lack of ability. However, if you continually, gradually pursue and gain knowledge of what you need to do, you will eliminate begging, because you'll know. You'll be fully equipped to possess what God has for you.

Wisdom is good with an inheritance: and by it there is profit to them that see the sun. For wisdom is a defence, and money is a defence: but the excellency of knowledge is, that wisdom giveth life to them that have it.

– Ecclesiastes 7:11–12

1882. Behavior possibly may change, but hearts rarely change, but by the grace of God.

The heart is deceitful above all things, and desperately wicked: who can know it? I the Lord search the heart, I try the reins, even to give every man according to his ways, and according to the fruit of his doings.

– Jeremiah 17:9–10

1883. Keep on praying, because, everyday anything is possible through the grace of God.

If my people, which are called by my name, shall humble themselves, and pray, and seek my face, and turn from their wicked ways; then will I hear from heaven, and will forgive their sin, and will heal their land.

–2 Chronicles 7:14

1884. To go through a day "prayer–less" is *perilous*!

And he spake a parable unto them *to this end*, that men ought always to pray, and not to faint.

– Luke 18:1

1885. Marriage is honorable, and the bed is undefiled; but whoremongers and adulterers God will judge. We should honor the marriage covenant between a man and a woman, and be faithful to our own spouses. Without faithfulness, husbands and wives violate and negate the force of their covenant, and cheat themselves out of the blessing upon their marriage.

Marriage is honorable in all, and the bed undefiled: but whoremongers and adulterers God will judge.

– Hebrews 13:4

1886. When God tells you to do something, just obey. It doesn't have to be pretty for it to be effective. If He tells you to do it, just quickly obey.

To do justice and judgment is more acceptable to the Lord than sacrifice.

– Proverbs 21:3

1887. A person that can control their own-self can control the world, and that scares some people.

He that is slow to anger is better than the mighty; and he that ruleth his spirit than he that taketh a city.

– Proverbs 16:32

1888. In regard to self-improvement, commit the cultivation of the godly virtues of your heart to God through the Word, prayer, worship, and fasting. Furthermore, commit the cultivation of your gifts and talents and skills to your own personal discipline and hard work.

And whatsoever ye do, do it heartily, as to the Lord, and not unto men; knowing that of the Lord ye shall receive the reward of the inheritance: for ye serve the Lord Christ.

– Colossians 3:23–24

1889. Make productivity a priority above publicity. Productivity is the key, because if you don't have anything to sell, then you don't have anything to promote. Make productivity a priority above publicity. *Get it done!*

Boast not thyself of to morrow; for thou knowest not what a day may bring forth.

– Proverbs 27:1

1890. Do a great job! And, congratulate yourself often. Because, often you may be your only cheerleader in the whole universe!

In the beginning God created the heaven and the earth. And the earth was without form, and void; and darkness was upon the face of the deep. And the Spirit of God moved upon the face of the waters. And God said, Let there be light: and there was light. And God saw the light, that it was good: and God divided the light from the darkness. And God called the light Day, and the darkness he called Night. And the evening and the morning were the first day. And God said, Let there be a firmament in the midst of the waters, and let it divide the waters from the waters. And God made the firmament, and divided the waters which were under the firmament from the waters which were above the firmament: and it was so. And God called the firmament Heaven. And the evening and the morning were the second day. And God said, Let the waters under the heaven be gathered together unto one place, and let the dry land appear: and it was so. And God called the dry land Earth; and the gathering together of the waters called he Seas: and God saw that it was good. And God said, Let the earth bring forth grass, the herb yielding seed, and the fruit tree yielding fruit after his kind, whose seed is in itself, upon the earth: and it was so. And the earth brought forth grass, and herb yielding seed after his kind, and the tree yielding fruit, whose seed was in itself, after his kind: and God saw that it was good. And the evening and the morning were the third day. And God said, Let there be lights in the firmament of the heaven to divide the day from the night; and let them be for signs, and for seasons, and for days, and years: And let them be for lights in the firmament of the heaven to give light upon the earth: and it was so. And God made two great lights; the greater light to rule the day, and the lesser light to rule the night: he made the stars also. And God set them in the firmament of the heaven to give light upon the earth, And to rule over the day and over the night, and to divide the light from the darkness: and God saw that it was good. And the evening and the morning were the fourth day. And God said, Let the waters bring forth abundantly the moving creature that hath life, and fowl that may fly above the earth in the open firmament of heaven. And God created great whales, and every living creature that moveth, which the waters brought forth abundantly, after their kind, and every winged fowl after his kind: and God saw that it was good. And God blessed them, saying, Be fruitful, and multiply, and fill the waters in the seas, and let fowl multiply in the earth. And the evening and the morning were the fifth day. And God said, Let the earth bring forth the living creature after his kind, cattle, and creeping thing, and beast of the earth after his kind: and it was so. And God made the beast of the earth after his kind, and cattle after their kind, and every thing that creepeth upon the earth after his kind: and God saw that it was good. And God said, Let us make man in our image, after our likeness: and let them have dominion over the fish of the sea, and over the fowl of the air, and over the cattle, and over all the earth, and over every creeping thing that creepeth upon the earth. So God created man in his own image, in the image of God created he him; male and female created he them. And God blessed them, and God said unto them, Be fruitful, and multiply, and replenish the earth, and subdue it: and have dominion over the fish of the sea, and over the fowl of the air, and over every living thing that moveth upon the earth. And God said, Behold, I have given you every herb bearing seed, which is upon the face of all the earth, and every tree, in the which is the fruit of a tree yielding seed; to you it shall be for meat. And to every beast of the earth, and to every fowl of the air, and to every thing that creepeth upon the earth, wherein there is life, I have given every green herb for meat: and it was so. And God saw every thing that he had made, and, behold, it was very good. And the evening and the morning were the sixth day.

– Genesis 1

But let every man prove his own work, and then shall he have rejoicing in himself alone, and not in another.

– Galatians 6:4

1891. The key to maintaining joy is to focus on the good, and to be thankful.

Rejoice in the Lord always: and again I say, Rejoice. Let your moderation be known unto all men. The Lord is at hand. Be careful for nothing; but in every thing by prayer and supplication with thanksgiving let your requests be made known unto God. And the peace of God, which passeth all understanding, shall keep your hearts and minds through Christ Jesus. Finally, brethren, whatsoever things are true, whatsoever things are honest, whatsoever things are just, whatsoever things are pure, whatsoever things are lovely, whatsoever things are of good report; if there be any virtue, and if there be any praise, think on these things. Those things, which ye have both learned, and received, and heard, and seen in me, do: and the God of peace shall be with you.

– Philippians 4:4–9

1892. There's safety in following in someone else's footsteps. However, it's better to have your own boots! Be interested. Be clear. Be careful. Be wise enough to strike out on your own path! Make your own footsteps. Make your own path. Follow others footsteps, but wear your *own boots*!

But when it pleased God, who separated me from my mothers womb, and called me by his grace, to reveal his Son in me, that I might preach him among the heathen; immediately I conferred not with flesh and blood: neither went I up to Jerusalem to them which were apostles before me; but I went into Arabia, and returned again unto Damascus. Then after three years I went up to Jerusalem to see Peter, and abode with him fifteen days. But other of the apostles saw I none, save James the Lord's brother.

– Galatians 1:15–19

1893. Be sober. Be vigilant. Don't let your emotions get the best of your head.

Humble yourselves therefore under the mighty hand of God, that he may exalt you in due time: Casting all your care upon him; for he careth for you. Be sober, be vigilant; because your adversary the devil, as a roaring lion, walketh about, seeking whom he may devour: Whom resist stedfast in the faith, knowing that the same afflictions are accomplished in your brethren that are in the world.

–1 Peter 5:6–9

1894. Without discipline, there is no release. Without the release of the anointing, there is no wealth!

What profit hath he that worketh in that wherein he laboureth? I have seen the travail, which God hath given to the sons of men to be exercised in it. He hath made every thing beautiful in his time: also he hath set the world in their heart, so that no man can find out the work that God maketh from the beginning to the end. I know that there is no good in them, but for a man to rejoice, and to do good in his life. And also that every man should eat and drink, and enjoy the good of all his labour, it is the gift of God.

– Ecclesiastes 3:9–13

1895. Vision provokes passion! Through passion purpose is obtained. Passion is the ignition for movement. Without movement nothing is accomplished.

Where there is no vision, the people perish: but he that keepeth the law, happy is he.

— Proverbs 29:18

1896. In regard to marriage and sex, your wife has the same things that the other woman has, but the other woman doesn't have the same thing that your wife has. That's why you married your wife.

Marriage is honorable in all, and the bed undefiled: but whoremongers and adulterers God will judge.

— Hebrews 13:4

Whoso findeth a wife findeth a good thing, and obtaineth favour of the Lord.

— Proverbs 18:22

1897. Some of the greatest blessings come out of service.

And Naomi had a kinsman of her husband's, a mighty man of wealth, of the family of Elimelech; and his name was Boaz. And Ruth the Moabitess said unto Naomi, Let me now go to the field, and glean ears of corn after him in whose sight I shall find grace. And she said unto her, Go, my daughter. And she went, and came, and gleaned in the field after the reapers: and her hap was to light on a part of the field belonging unto Boaz, who was of the kindred of Elimelech. And, behold, Boaz came from Bethlehem, and said unto the reapers, The Lord be with you. And they answered him, The Lord bless thee. Then said Boaz unto his servant that was set over the reapers, Whose damsel is this? And the servant that was set over the reapers answered and said, It is the Moabitish damsel that came back with Naomi out of the country of Moab: And she said, I pray you, let me glean and gather after the reapers among the sheaves: so she came, and hath continued even from the morning until now, that she tarried a little in the house. Then said Boaz unto Ruth, Hearest thou not, my daughter? Go not to glean in another field, neither go from hence, but abide here fast by my maidens: Let thine eyes be on the field that they do reap, and go thou after them: have I not charged the young men that they shall not touch thee? and when thou art athirst, go unto the vessels, and drink of that which the young men have drawn. Then she fell on her face, and bowed herself to the ground, and said unto him, Why have I found grace in thine eyes, that thou shouldest take knowledge of me, seeing I am a stranger? And Boaz answered and said unto her, It hath fully been shewed me, all that thou hast done unto thy mother in law since the death of thine husband: and how thou hast left thy father and thy mother, and the land of thy nativity, and art come unto a people which thou knewest not heretofore. The Lord recompense thy work, and a full reward be given thee of the Lord God of Israel, under whose wings thou art come to trust. Then she said, Let me find favour in thy sight, my lord; for that thou hast comforted me, and for that thou hast spoken friendly unto thine handmaid, though I be not like unto one of thine handmaidens. And Boaz said unto her, At mealtime come thou hither, and eat of the bread, and dip thy morsel in the vinegar. And she sat beside the reapers: and he reached her parched corn, and she did eat, and was sufficed, and left. And when she was risen up to glean, Boaz commanded his young men, saying, Let her glean even among the sheaves, and reproach her not: And let fall also some of the handfuls of purpose for her, and leave them, that she may glean them, and rebuke her not. So she gleaned in the field until even, and beat out that she had gleaned: and it was about an ephah of barley. And she took it up, and went into the city: and her mother in law saw what she had gleaned: and she brought forth, and gave to her that she had reserved after she was sufficed. And her mother in law said unto her, Where hast thou gleaned to day? and where wroughtest thou? blessed be he that did take knowledge of thee. And she shewed her mother in law with whom she had wrought, and said, The man's name with whom I wrought to day is Boaz. And Naomi said unto her daughter in law, Blessed be he of the Lord, who hath not left off his kindness to the living and to the dead. And Naomi said unto her, The man is near of kin unto us, one of our next kinsmen. And Ruth the Moabitess said, He said unto me also, Thou shalt keep fast by my young men, until they have ended all my harvest. And Naomi said unto Ruth her daughter in law, It is good, my daughter, that thou go out with his maidens, that they meet thee not in any other field. So she kept fast by the maidens of Boaz to glean unto the end of barley harvest and of wheat harvest; and dwelt with her mother in law.

– Ruth 2

1898. Neither give place to the devil. Don't give him any room when you see a storm rising. Whether the storm is in the natural weather or in the spiritual, resist the devil. Bind that storm immediately! Rebuke the devil! Put him in his place. Put him under your feet! Command him to run! Command him to leave! Don't give room to the devil. Don't allow him to get strong. Bind him at the start.

Neither give place to the devil.

– Ephesians 4:27

1899. The best way to mark your calendar is through achieved goals. Keep your calendar full, by setting high, achievable goals, and keeping on achieving them!

Say not ye, There are yet four months, and then cometh harvest? behold, I say unto you, Lift up your eyes, and look on the fields; for they are white already to harvest.

– John 4:35

So teach us to number our days, that we may apply our hearts unto wisdom.

– Psalm 90:12

1900. God has added his special seasoning to each unique combination of the egg and seed that has come together to form the billions of people throughout the history of mankind's existence, and He has never combined the spices quite the same twice! That's what makes you special and uniquely you! You are a once in an eternity special flavor of God's creative love! What a wonderful God we serve! His wonders are too numerous to comprehend!

I will praise thee; for I am fearfully and wonderfully made: marvellous are thy works; and that my soul knoweth right well. My substance was not hid from thee, when I was made in secret, and curiously wrought in the lowest parts of the earth. Thine eyes did see my substance, yet being unperfect; and in thy book all my members were written, which in continuance were fashioned, when as yet there was none of them. How precious also are thy thoughts unto me, O God! how great is the sum of them! If I should count them, they are more in number than the sand: when I awake, I am still with thee.

– Psalm 139:14–18

1901. God wants to bless us, so that we'll help Him accomplish His purpose in the earth. We deprive Him of pleasure, and hinder His plan, when we fail to achieve.

Let them shout for joy, and be glad, that favour my righteous cause: yea, let them say continually, Let the Lord be magnified, which hath pleasure in the prosperity of his servant.

– Psalm 35:27

1902. The only thing that stands between you and your greatest dreams coming true is *work*. The only thing that stands between you doing the work to obtain your greatest dreams is your *willingness* to do the work. "If you be willing and obedient, you shall eat the good of the land!"

If ye be willing and obedient, ye shall eat the good of the land.

143

– Isaiah 1:19

If they obey and serve him, they shall spend their days in prosperity, and their years in pleasures.

– Job 36:11

1903. Unbroken focus is the key to your ultimate financial success. Unending distractions are the keys to your eventual financial destruction.

Through desire a man, having separated himself, seeketh and intermeddleth with all wisdom.

– Proverbs 18:1

But his delight is in the law of the Lord; and in his law doth he meditate day and night. And he shall be like a tree planted by the rivers of water, that bringeth forth his fruit in his season; his leaf also shall not wither; and whatsoever he doeth shall prosper.

– Psalm 1:2–3

1904. *"I do"* are powerful words. They're as powerful as you make them.

And he answered and said unto them, Have ye not read, that he which made them at the beginning made them male and female, and said, For this cause shall a man leave father and mother, and shall cleave to his wife: and they twain shall be one flesh? Wherefore they are no more twain, but one flesh.

What therefore God hath joined together, let not man put asunder.

— Matthew 19:4–6

1905. As a *nice* person, always be aware that there's someone trying to take advantage of you. Therefore, you must be as wise as the criminal, yet, live as a saint. In other words, be aware of how the criminal thinks, yet, live as a saint. Thus, you will avoid being taken advantage of. Jesus said, "Be wise as a serpent, but harmless as a dove."

Behold, I send you forth as sheep in the midst of wolves: be ye therefore wise as serpents, and harmless as doves.

— Matthew 10:16

1906. In business and in life, you cannot lie back on the beach and expect someone to *feed you grapes*! No! You have to go into your promised land, and cut down the grapes! Even if you have to bring them out on a staff on your shoulder! The grapes are large, but you have to fight for them! You have to *take* the land! God has given it to you! Go in at once, and possess it!

So they went up, and searched the land from the wilderness of Zin unto Rehob, as men come to Hamath. And they ascended by the south, and came unto Hebron; where Ahiman, Sheshai, and Talmai, the children of Anak, were. (Now Hebron was built seven years before Zoan in Egypt.) And they came unto the brook of Eshcol, and cut down from thence a branch with one cluster of grapes, and they bare it between two upon a staff; and they brought of the pomegranates, and of the figs. The place was called the brook Eshcol, because of the cluster of grapes which the children of Israel cut down from thence.

– Numbers 13:21–24

And Caleb stilled the people before Moses, and said, Let us go up at once, and possess it; for we are well able to overcome it.

– Numbers 13:30

1907. The Holy Spirit is the *"Anointing."* The anointing is an expression of the Holy Spirit. The anointing is the empowerment to do beyond what your natural strength can do.

But ye have an unction from the Holy One, and ye know all things.

–1 John 2:20

But the anointing which ye have received of him abideth in you, and ye need not that any man teach you: but as the same anointing teacheth you of all things, and is truth, and is no lie, and even as it hath taught you, ye shall abide in him.

–1 John 2:27

1908. Without truth even success is devoid of lasting confidence.

For what is a man profited, if he shall gain the whole world, and lose his own soul? or what shall a man give in exchange for his soul?

– Matthew 16:26

1909. In regard to life, you may want to *"tiptoe through the tulips"*, but you better wear some shoes. Life can be thorny!

Behold, I send you forth as sheep in the midst of wolves: be ye therefore wise as serpents, and harmless as doves.

– Matthew 10:16

1910. Living food keeps you alive. Dead food makes you die earlier. Always evaluate what you eat by asking, "Is it alive or is it dead?" Then, you will know how it will affect you. Feed your body and soul *living* food. Feast on God's Word, and eat healthy food. You will have *"life, and life more abundantly!"*

And God said, Behold, I have given you every herb bearing seed, which is upon the face of all the earth, and every tree, in the which is the fruit of a tree yielding seed; to you it shall be for meat.

– Genesis 1:29

A man's belly shall be satisfied with the fruit of his mouth; and with the increase of his lips shall he be filled. Death and life are in the power of the tongue: and they that love it shall eat the fruit thereof.

– Proverbs 18:20–21

The thief cometh not, but for to steal, and to kill, and to destroy: I am come that they might have life, and that they might have it more abundantly.

– John 10:10

1911. May you be kept in perfect peace as your mind is staid continually upon the Lord. Trust in the Lord forever, for in the Lord Jehovah you will find everlasting strength! Have a blessed weekend!

Thou wilt keep him in perfect peace, whose mind is stayed on thee: because he trusteth in thee. Trust ye in the Lord for ever: for in the Lord JEHOVAH is everlasting strength.

– Isaiah 26:3–4

1912. Let everything that has breath praise the Lord for what He has done for each of us! It doesn't take a lot to be thankful. It just takes a willing mind and a grateful heart. Give God praise daily for what He has done for you!

Let every thing that hath breath praise the Lord. Praise ye the Lord.

– Psalm 150:6

It is a good thing to give thanks unto the Lord, and to sing praises unto thy name, O Most High: To shew forth thy

lovingkindness in the morning, and thy faithfulness every night.

– Psalm 92:1–2

1913. Everyone is a *"star"* in someone else's sky. So, shine while you can. Make the most of your days and nights. Shine as bright as the Sun in the day. Give direction and guidance as the North Star in someone's night. Let your light so very much shine! You are the *star* in someone else's sky!

Ye are the salt of the earth: but if the salt have lost his savour, wherewith shall it be salted? it is thenceforth good for nothing, but to be cast out, and to be trodden under foot of men. Ye are the light of the world. A city that is set on an hill cannot be hid. Neither do men light a candle, and put it under a bushel, but on a candlestick; and it giveth light unto all that are in the house. Let your light so shine before men, that they may see your good works, and glorify your Father which is in heaven.

– Matthew 5:13–16

1914. Have a *"spiritual sandwich"* everyday. Have a time of morning devotion and an evening devotion. Talk to the Lord and praise Him in the middle of the day. You will never go hungry. You will be filled with the Spirit daily. Have a "spiritual sandwich" daily. It's *"Um, um, good!"*

It is a good thing to give thanks unto the Lord, and to sing praises unto thy name, O Most High: To shew forth thy

lovingkindness in the morning, and thy faithfulness every night.

– Psalm 92:1–2

And in the morning, rising up a great while before day, he went out, and departed into a solitary place, and there prayed.

– Mark 1:35

And straightway Jesus constrained his disciples to get into a ship, and to go before him unto the other side, while he sent the multitudes away. And when he had sent the multitudes away, he went up into a mountain apart to pray: and when the evening was come, he was there alone.

– Matthew 14:22–23

1915. God is pleased with you today! You are the highlight of Heaven. Every morning you wake up He delights in you. He takes pleasure in your progress, and He takes pleasure in prospering you. You are the highlight of Heaven today! Praise God! Now, take a moment to *personalize* this truth. Acknowledge it. You will feel just how special you are to God, your Heavenly Father. Embrace His love for you!

Blessed be the God and Father of our Lord Jesus Christ, who hath blessed us with all spiritual blessings in heavenly places in Christ: According as he hath chosen us in him before the foundation of the world, that we should be holy and without blame before him in love: Having predestinated us unto the adoption of children by Jesus Christ to himself, according to the good pleasure of his will, To the praise of the glory of his grace, wherein he hath made us accepted in the beloved.

– Ephesians 1:3–6

1916. Singing praise and worship to God clears out all of the *cobwebs* out of your mind and heart. Make room for the Holy Ghost. Sing praise and worship onto God.

Make a joyful noise unto the Lord, all ye lands. Serve the Lord with gladness: come before his presence with singing. Know ye that the Lord he is God: it is he that hath made us, and not we ourselves; we are his people, and the sheep of his pasture. Enter into his gates with thanksgiving, and into his courts with praise: be thankful unto him, and bless his name. For the Lord is good; his mercy is everlasting; and his truth endureth to all generations.

– Psalm 100

1917. Singing daily is an *attitude lifter!*

A merry heart doeth good like a medicine: but a broken spirit drieth the bones.

– Proverbs 17:22

1918. Death is downward. Life is upward! Choose life! Choose to have a positive attitude. Think up! Speak up! Get up! And be up! Choose life. Choose a positive attitude.

I call heaven and earth to record this day against you, that I have set before you life and death, blessing and cursing: therefore choose life, that both thou and thy seed may live.

– Deuteronomy 30:19

1919. If God is able to bring you up, He's able to keep you up. It was Him that brought you up. Don't be afraid of whether success can last. If God brings you up, then He can keep you up all the days of your life!

And the Lord turned the captivity of Job, when he prayed for his friends: also the Lord gave Job twice as much as he had before. Then came there unto him all his brethren, and all his sisters, and all they that had been of his acquaintance before, and did eat bread with him in his house: and they bemoaned him, and comforted him over all the evil that the Lord had brought upon him: every man also gave him a piece of money, and every one an earring of gold. So the Lord blessed the latter end of Job more than his beginning: for he had fourteen thousand sheep, and six thousand camels, and a thousand yoke of oxen, and a thousand she asses. He had also seven sons and three daughters. And he called the name of the first, Jemima; and the name of the second, Kezia; and the name of the third, Kerenhappuch. And in all the land were no women found so fair as the daughters of Job: and their father gave them inheritance among their brethren. After this lived Job an hundred and forty years, and saw his sons, and his sons sons, even four generations. So Job died, being old and full of days.

– Job 42:10–17

1920. Regarding your field of dreams, you can't guarantee that if you build it, they will come, but you can guarantee that if you *don't* build it they won't come. Pursue your dreams. Take the *chance*. You only have one life to live. All successful people pursued their dreams!

Whatsoever thy hand findeth to do, do it with thy might; for there is no work, nor device, nor knowledge, nor wisdom, in the grave, whither thou goest. I returned, and saw under the sun, that the race is not to the swift, nor the battle to the strong, neither yet bread to the wise, nor yet riches to men of understanding, nor yet favour to men of skill; but time and chance happeneth to them all.

– Ecclesiastes 9:10–11

1921. One thing is for sure: *sisters* know how to adapt and thrive! Your wealth is in your ability to use what God has put in you to thrive in the good times and bad. Your diligent implementation of the anointing will destroy the yoke of impossibly off of your life. You will thrive, and not just survive!

Now there cried a certain woman of the wives of the sons of the prophets unto Elisha, saying, Thy servant my husband is dead; and thou knowest that thy servant did fear the Lord: and the creditor is come to take unto him my two sons to be bondmen. And Elisha said unto her, What shall I do for thee? tell me, what hast thou in the house? And she said, Thine handmaid hath not any thing in the house, save a pot of oil. Then he said, Go, borrow thee vessels abroad of all thy neighbours, even empty vessels; borrow not a few. And when thou art come in, thou shalt shut the door upon thee and upon thy sons, and shalt pour out into all those vessels, and thou shalt set aside that which is full. So she went from him, and shut the door upon her and upon her sons, who brought the vessels to her; and she poured out. And it came to pass, when the vessels were full, that she said unto her son, Bring me yet a vessel. And he said unto her, There is not a vessel more. And the oil stayed. Then she came and told the man of God. And he said, Go, sell the oil, and pay thy debt, and live thou and thy children of the rest.

–2 Kings 4:1–7

1922. Who has ears to hear? Let them hear: you were born on purpose. You were born with a purpose. You are a significant *shift* that has changed the direction of the future of history! Now, fulfill yourself!

For if thou altogether holdest thy peace at this time, then shall there enlargement and deliverance arise to the Jews from another place; but thou and thy fathers house shall be destroyed: and who knoweth whether thou art come to the kingdom for such a time as this?

– Esther 4:14

1923. Some characteristics are a matter of personality. Some characteristics are a matter of *refinement*. Success requires refinement of our personalities.

Behold, I have refined thee, but not with silver; I have chosen thee in the furnace of affliction.

– Isaiah 48:10

1924. I pray that you will have *1000 days* of good news, and no bad news. The only bad news that you will have is that there is no bad news. Thus, the bad news is better than the good news.

As cold waters to a thirsty soul, so is good news from a far country.

– Proverbs 25:25

1925. Insecurity has a *sound*. It's called criticism.

He that is despised, and hath a servant, is better than he that honoureth himself, and lacketh bread.

– Proverbs 12:9

1926. Determination, patience, and persistence are the keys to success. Determine your desired destination. Be patient in the process. Persist to the end, and you will obtain success.

That ye be not slothful, but followers of them who through faith and patience inherit the promises.

– Hebrews 6:12

1927. Workers get paid by the hour. *Producers* get paid by the product. Workers earn a wage. Producers earn *wealth*.

In the morning sow thy seed, and in the evening withhold not thine hand: for thou knowest not whether shall prosper, either this or that, or whether they both shall be alike good.

– Ecclesiastes 11:6

1928. Happiness is a weapon.

Then he said unto them, Go your way, eat the fat, and drink the sweet, and send portions unto them for whom nothing is prepared: for this day is holy unto our Lord: neither be ye sorry; for the joy of the Lord is your strength.

– Nehemiah 8:10

1929. No matter how your critics try to fight you, always know that no one can fight what God has ordained. If God said, "Yes", who else matters?

And Stephen, full of faith and power, did great wonders and miracles among the people. Then there arose certain of the synagogue, which is called the synagogue of the Libertines, and Cyrenians, and Alexandrians, and of them of Cilicia and of Asia, disputing with Stephen. And they were not able to resist the wisdom and the spirit by which he spake.

– Acts 6:8–10

To subvert a man in his cause, the Lord approveth not. Who is he that saith, and it cometh to pass, when the Lord commandeth it not? Out of the mouth of the most High proceedeth not evil and good?

– Lamentations 3:36–38

1930. Take all opportunities that advance you in the right direction.

Whatsoever thy hand findeth to do, do it with thy might; for there is no work, nor device, nor knowledge, nor wisdom, in the grave, whither thou goest. I returned, and saw under the sun, that the race is not to the swift, nor the battle to the strong, neither yet bread to the wise, nor yet riches to men of understanding, nor yet favour to men of skill; but time and chance happeneth to them all.

– Ecclesiastes 9:10–11

1931. In our busy world, sometimes the years, faces, and places may seem to all run together, but God's Word stays the same. Live your life by God's unchanging principles. Love people. Live on purpose. Rejoice always. You will end up living a *memorable* life!

For to him that is joined to all the living there is hope: for a living dog is better than a dead lion. For the living know that they shall die: but the dead know not any thing, neither have they any more a reward; for the memory of them is forgotten. Also their love, and their hatred, and their envy, is now perished; neither have they any more a portion for ever in any thing that is done under the sun. Go thy way, eat thy bread with joy, and drink thy wine with a merry heart; for God now accepteth thy works. Let thy garments be always white; and let thy head lack no ointment. Live joyfully with the wife whom thou lovest all the days of the life of thy vanity, which he hath given thee under the sun, all the days of thy vanity: for that is thy portion in this life, and in thy labour which thou takest under the sun. Whatsoever thy hand findeth to do, do it with thy might; for there is no work, nor device, nor knowledge, nor wisdom, in the grave, whither thou goest. I returned, and saw under the sun, that the race is not to the swift, nor the battle to the strong, neither yet bread to the wise, nor yet riches to men of understanding, nor yet favour to men of skill; but time and chance happeneth to them all.

– Ecclesiastes 9:4–11

1932. You can't detect whether a man will be faithful or not, because faithfulness is a *"moment by moment"* commitment. A man must be intentional about being faithful. He must be continually seeking God and God's strength, because "the spirit is willing, but the flesh is weak", and we are all in these fleshly bodies. Therefore, we all need God in order for us to stay faithful. However, you can detect tendencies toward faithfulness, and you can possibly guess about who will be faithful, based on past behavior, training, and the nature of their personality.

Most men will proclaim every one his own goodness: but a faithful man who can find?

– Proverbs 20:6

1933. Life takes courage.

Be strong and courageous, be not afraid nor dismayed for the king of Assyria, nor for all the multitude that is with him: for there be more with us than with him: with him is an arm of flesh; but with us is the Lord our God to help us, and to fight our battles. And the people rested themselves upon the words of Hezekiah king of Judah.

–2 Chronicles 32:7–8

1934. Regarding money, excitement leads to spending. Patience leads to planning. Be strategic in your use of money. It will lead to an exciting result!

Wilt thou set thine eyes upon that which is not? for riches certainly make themselves wings; they fly away as an eagle toward heaven.

– Proverbs 23:5

Be thou diligent to know the state of thy flocks, and look well to thy herds. For riches are not for ever: and doth the crown endure to every generation? The hay appeareth, and the tender grass sheweth itself, and herbs of the mountains are gathered. The lambs are for thy clothing, and the goats are the price of the field. And thou shalt have goats milk enough for thy food, for the food of thy household, and for the maintenance for thy maidens.

– Proverbs 27:23–27

1935. Pay for advisement, but keep your own counsel.

But when it pleased God, who separated me from my mothers womb, and called me by his grace, to reveal his Son in me, that I might preach him among the heathen; immediately I conferred not with flesh and blood: neither went I up to Jerusalem to them which were apostles before me; but I went into Arabia, and returned again unto Damascus. Then after three years I went up to Jerusalem to see Peter, and abode with him fifteen days. But other of the apostles saw I none, save James the Lord's brother.

– Galatians 1:15–19

1936. Always remember, you are the CEO of your own life. Pay for advice, but don't lose your status.

And now, behold, I go bound in the spirit unto Jerusalem, not knowing the things that shall befall me there: Save that the Holy Ghost witnesseth in every city, saying that bonds and afflictions abide me. But none of these things move me, neither count I my life dear unto myself, so that I might finish my course with joy, and the ministry, which I have received of the Lord Jesus, to testify the gospel of the grace of God.

– Acts 20:22–24

1937. Even a rattlesnake will slow down long enough for you to pet and comfort it when it's sick. But, don't fail to listen for the *moving of its rattle again*!

Behold, I send you forth as sheep in the midst of wolves: be ye therefore wise as serpents, and harmless as doves.

– Matthew 10:16

1938. Ideas and concepts are how the *"West was won"*, and how business is run. Take time to appraise the tremendous creative and monetary value of your own ideas and concepts, and don't allow yourself to be swindled, hornswoggled, or bamboozled by others who will readily relieve you of the value you have produced if you fail to protect and make use of it yourself.

It is naught, it is naught, saith the buyer: but when he is gone his way, then he boasteth.

– Proverbs 20:14

1939. Excitement begets spending. Patience begets planning.

The simple believeth every word: but the prudent man looketh well to his going.

– Proverbs 14:15

1940. The way to succeed is to start with a burning, grand vision. Then, keep taking the necessary steps towards its fulfillment. It becomes clearer and clearer, as you take actions towards it. Then, seemingly, suddenly, it will appear into full view, as if it always existed. And, it did. The only thing that changed was you. As the vision manifested, it revealed a higher level of *you* to yourself!

For the earnest expectation of the creature waiteth for the manifestation of the sons of God.

– Romans 8:19

1941. When the saints prevail in prayer, the saints will *prevail.*

I exhort therefore, that, first of all, supplications, prayers, intercessions, and giving of thanks, be made for all men; For kings, and for all that are in authority; that we may lead a quiet and peaceable life in all godliness and honesty.

–1 Timothy 2:1–2

1942. The best way to make money is to *not spend* money. There's a difference between an expense and an investment. Expenses are *spent*. Investments are a vested interest into

162

your future. Invest money and reduce the instances of spending money, and thus, you will *make* money.

Cast thy bread upon the waters: for thou shalt find it after many days. Give a portion to seven, and also to eight; for thou knowest not what evil shall be upon the earth. If the clouds be full of rain, they empty themselves upon the earth: and if the tree fall toward the south, or toward the north, in the place where the tree falleth, there it shall be. He that observeth the wind shall not sow; and he that regardeth the clouds shall not reap. As thou knowest not what is the way of the spirit, nor how the bones do grow in the womb of her that is with child: even so thou knowest not the works of God who maketh all. In the morning sow thy seed, and in the evening withhold not thine hand: for thou knowest not whether shall prosper, either this or that, or whether they both shall be alike good.

– Ecclesiastes 11:1–6

1943. Invest your money to make more money. Don't just spend money randomly.

Be thou diligent to know the state of thy flocks, and look well to thy herds. For riches are not for ever: and doth the crown endure to every generation? The hay appeareth, and the tender grass sheweth itself, and herbs of the mountains are gathered. The lambs are for thy clothing, and the goats are the price of the field. And thou shalt have goats milk enough for thy food, for the food of thy household, and for the maintenance for thy maidens.

– Proverbs 27:23–27

1944. Don't start spending before you start *counting*!

Wilt thou set thine eyes upon that which is not? for riches certainly make themselves wings; they fly away as an eagle toward heaven.

– Proverbs 23:5

1945. Don't worry about the time that it takes to do what's required to obtain what's desired. Progress is progressive.

The steps of a good man are ordered by the Lord: and he delighteth in his way.

– Psalm 37:23

1946. Life is full of reality. It's good to have a dream. The just shall live by his or her faith!

And the Lord answered me, and said, Write the vision, and make it plain upon tables, that he may run that readeth it. For the vision is yet for an appointed time, but at the end it shall speak, and not lie: though it tarry, wait for it; because it will surely come, it will not tarry. Behold, his soul which is lifted up is not upright in him: but the just shall live by his faith.

– Habakkuk 2:2–4

1947. Be wise as a serpent, but don't *become* one!

Behold, I send you forth as sheep in the midst of wolves: be ye therefore wise as serpents, and harmless as doves.

– Matthew 10:16

Brethren, be not children in understanding: howbeit in malice be ye children, but in understanding be men.

–1 Corinthians 14:20

1948. Live today by your work. Live *forever* by your words.

For all flesh is as grass, and all the glory of man as the flower of grass. The grass withereth, and the flower thereof falleth away: But the word of the Lord endureth for ever. And this is the word which by the gospel is preached unto you.

–1 Peter 1:24–25

1949. Life is a trip! Your attitude will determine how you take it!

All the days of the afflicted are evil: but he that is of a merry heart hath a continual feast.

– Proverbs 15:15

1950. Happiness and joy are a matter of choice. It's a matter of attitude. It's a matter of the heart. It's not a matter of the circumstances. Don't let anything or anyone take your joy. Happiness is a matter of the heart. It's not a matter of the circumstances.

My brethren, count it all joy when ye fall into divers temptations; Knowing this, that the trying of your faith worketh patience. But let patience have her perfect work, that ye may be perfect and entire, wanting nothing.

– James 1:2–4

1951. Regarding relationships, an apology never changes a person's *nature*. Only prayer and grace can do that.

For the word of God is quick, and powerful, and sharper than any twoedged sword, piercing even to the dividing asunder of soul and spirit, and of the joints and marrow, and is a discerner of the thoughts and intents of the heart. Neither is there any creature that is not manifest in his sight: but all things are naked and opened unto the eyes of him with whom we have to do. Seeing then that we have a great high priest, that is passed into the heavens, Jesus the Son of God, let us hold fast our profession. For we have not an high priest which cannot be touched with the feeling of our infirmities; but was in all points tempted like as we are, yet without sin. Let us therefore come boldly unto the throne of grace, that we may obtain mercy, and find grace to help in time of need.

– Hebrews 4:12–16

1952. You're paid to solve problems. So, if you run away from problems, you run away from your *paycheck*.

And whatsoever ye do, do it heartily, as to the Lord, and not unto men; knowing that of the Lord ye shall receive the reward of the inheritance: for ye serve the Lord Christ.

– Colossians 3:23–24

1953. The willingness to go to any lawful extreme is the price of extreme success.

For though I be free from all men, yet have I made myself servant unto all, that I might gain the more. And unto the Jews I became as a Jew, that I might gain the Jews; to them that are under the law, as under the law, that I might gain them that are under the law; To them that are without law, as without law, (being not without law to God, but under the law to Christ,) that I might gain them that are without law. To the weak became I as weak, that I might gain the weak: I am made all things to all men, that I might by all means save some.

–1 Corinthians 9:19–22

1954. Drown out the voices of adversaries, opposition, and criticism by the force of your productivity. They may continue to talk, but you will no longer be distracted by their influence, because you will be too absorbed in succeeding. Just keep on producing!

But let every man prove his own work, and then shall he have rejoicing in himself alone, and not in another.

– Galatians 6:4

1955. Keep sowing seed toward the future, and you will have both a future and a harvest.

Cast thy bread upon the waters: for thou shalt find it after many days. Give a portion to seven, and also to eight; for thou knowest not what evil shall be upon the earth. If the clouds be full of rain, they empty themselves upon the earth: and if the tree fall toward the south, or toward the north, in the place where the tree falleth, there it shall be. He that observeth the wind shall not sow; and he that regardeth the clouds shall not reap. As thou knowest not what is the way of the spirit, nor how the bones do grow in the womb of her that is with child: even so thou knowest not the works of God who maketh all. In the morning sow thy seed, and in the evening withhold not thine hand: for thou knowest not whether shall prosper, either this or that, or whether they both shall be alike good.

– Ecclesiastes 11:1–6

1956. Regarding business, no single company or organization fully owns the entire market. Otherwise, they wouldn't continue marketing. Often, as a means of deterring others from entering the market, individual companies will attempt to make you think that they own the entire market, but if they owned the entire market, they wouldn't continue marketing.

It is naught, it is naught, saith the buyer: but when he is gone his way, then he boasteth.

– Proverbs 20:14

But rather seek ye the kingdom of God; and all these things shall be added unto you. Fear not, little flock; for it is your Fathers good pleasure to give you the kingdom. Sell that ye have, and give alms; provide yourselves bags which wax not old, a treasure in the heavens that faileth not, where no thief approacheth, neither moth corrupteth. For where your treasure is, there will your heart be also.

– Luke 12:31–34

1957. Don't fight getting older. Rather, focus on getting better every day of every year. Live everyday with intentionality, so that you are daily fulfilling your God-given purpose. You will then have a greater sense of satisfaction as the years go by.

So teach us to number our days, that we may apply our hearts unto wisdom.

– Psalm 90:12

1958. Insist on being the best, and make no allowances for the lower part of your nature.

I therefore, the prisoner of the Lord, beseech you that ye walk worthy of the vocation wherewith ye are called, with all lowliness and meekness, with longsuffering, forbearing one another in love; endeavouring to keep the unity of the Spirit in the bond of peace.

– Ephesians 4:1–3

Brethren, I count not myself to have apprehended: but this one thing I do, forgetting those things which are behind, and reaching forth unto those things which are before, I press toward the mark for the prize of the high calling of God in Christ Jesus.

– Philippians 3:13–14

1959. Everybody needs to stand on their own two feet if they can, because the resistance of standing builds strength. If nothing is wrong with you, you need to continue to stand, if you can. This includes physical, mental, moral, spiritual, and financial. Having done all to stand, *stand*!

Finally, my brethren, be strong in the Lord, and in the power of his might. Put on the whole armour of God, that ye may be able to stand against the wiles of the devil. For we wrestle not against flesh and blood, but against principalities, against powers, against the rulers of the darkness of this world, against spiritual wickedness in high places. Wherefore take unto you the whole armour of God, that ye may be able to withstand in the evil day, and having done all, to stand. Stand therefore, having your loins girt about with truth, and having on the breastplate of righteousness; And your feet shod with the preparation of the gospel of peace; Above all, taking the shield of faith, wherewith ye shall be able to quench all the fiery darts of the wicked. And take the helmet of salvation, and the sword of the Spirit, which is the word of God: Praying always with all prayer and supplication in the Spirit, and watching thereunto with all perseverance and supplication for all saints.

– Ephesians 6:10–18

1960. Regarding business, business is not black–and–white. Business is *green*.

A feast is made for laughter, and wine maketh merry: but money answereth all things.

– Ecclesiastes 10:19

1961. It pays to live right. It pays to live holy. It pays to live for Jesus Christ as Lord and Savior, because when it gets all the way down to the *"nitty-gritty"*, I just want to see that *Golden city*!

And he carried me away in the spirit to a great and high mountain, and shewed me that great city, the holy Jerusalem, descending out of heaven from God, Having the glory of God: and her light was like unto a stone most precious, even like a jasper stone, clear as crystal; And had a wall great and high, and had twelve gates, and at the gates twelve angels, and names written thereon, which are the names of the twelve tribes of the children of Israel: On the east three gates; on the north three gates; on the south three gates; and on the west three gates. And the wall of the city had twelve foundations, and in them the names of the twelve apostles of the Lamb. And he that talked with me had a golden reed to measure the city, and the gates thereof, and the wall thereof. And the city lieth foursquare, and the length is as large as the breadth: and he measured the city with the reed, twelve thousand furlongs. The length and the breadth and the height of it are equal. And he measured the wall thereof, an hundred and forty and four cubits, according to the measure of a man, that is, of the angel. And the building of the wall of it was of jasper: and the city was pure gold, like unto clear glass. And the foundations of the wall of the city were garnished with all manner of precious stones. The first foundation was jasper; the second, sapphire; the third, a chalcedony; the fourth, an emerald; The fifth, sardonyx; the sixth, sardius; the seventh, chrysolyte; the eighth, beryl; the ninth, a topaz; the tenth, a chrysoprasus; the eleventh, a jacinth; the twelfth, an amethyst. And the twelve gates were twelve pearls: every several gate was of one pearl: and the street of the city was pure gold, as it were transparent glass.

– Revelation 21:10–21

1962. The Lord is working on your behalf. The future is brighter than you may now perceive. Keep looking up. The Sun is shining in your direction!

But unto you that fear my name shall the Sun of righteousness arise with healing in his wings; and ye shall go forth, and grow up as calves of the stall.

– Malachi 4:2

1963. The truth is never intimidated by a lie. The truth is the truth. It cannot lie. The truth is the truth. It can't be denied. The truth is never intimidated by a lie.

The lip of truth shall be established for ever: but a lying tongue is but for a moment.

– Proverbs 12:19

1964. Don't stress–out. Rather, press into prayer.

And he spake a parable unto them *to this end*, that men ought always to pray, and not to faint.

– Luke 18:1

1965. Sincere appreciation is always appreciated.

And it came to pass, as he went to Jerusalem, that he passed through the midst of Samaria and Galilee. And as he entered into a certain village, there met him ten men that were lepers, which stood afar off: And they lifted up their voices, and said, Jesus, Master, have mercy on us. And when he saw them, he said unto them, Go shew yourselves unto the priests. And it came to pass, that, as they went, they were cleansed. And one of them, when he saw that he was healed, turned back, and with a loud voice glorified God, And fell down on his face at his feet, giving him thanks: and he was a Samaritan. And Jesus answering said, Were there not ten cleansed? but where are the nine? There are not found that returned to give glory to God, save this stranger. And he said unto him, Arise, go thy way: thy faith hath made thee whole.

– Luke 17:11–19

1966. If it can be done, it should be done. You don't know what can be done, until you try. Don't say what can't be done, until you try. If it can be done, it should be done. You can do it!

I can do all things through Christ, which strengtheneth me.

– Philippians 4:13

1967. Wherever you are, you should learn something.

Without counsel purposes are disappointed: but in the multitude of counsellors they are established.

– Proverbs 15:22

1968. It pays to be prepared and prompt. It costs to be lax and late.

Then shall the kingdom of heaven be likened unto ten virgins, which took their lamps, and went forth to meet the bridegroom. And five of them were wise, and five were foolish. They that were foolish took their lamps, and took no oil with them: but the wise took oil in their vessels with their lamps. While the bridegroom tarried, they all slumbered and slept. And at midnight there was a cry made, Behold, the bridegroom cometh; go ye out to meet him. Then all those virgins arose, and trimmed their lamps. And the foolish said unto the wise, Give us of your oil; for our lamps are gone out. But the wise answered, saying, Not so; lest there be not enough for us and you: but go ye rather to them that sell, and buy for yourselves. And while they went to buy, the bridegroom came; and they that were ready went in with him to the marriage: and the door was shut. Afterward came also the other virgins, saying, Lord, Lord, open to us. But he answered and said, Verily I say unto you, I know you not. Watch therefore, for ye know neither the day nor the hour wherein the Son of man cometh.

– Matthew 25:1–13

1969. Regarding rest, even the Sun goes down at the end of the day. Take time to get your rest.

And he said unto them, Come ye yourselves apart into a desert place, and rest a while: for there were many coming and going, and they had no leisure so much as to eat.

– Mark 6:31

1970. Once you make the decision to solve a problem, it's no longer a problem. It becomes a challenge. Go forward courageously with the commitment to address the challenge. You will win as the champion! Life is full of opportunities to show that you are a champion. Every time you take on the challenge, you will gain a crown.

I have fought a good fight, I have finished my course, I have kept the faith: henceforth there is laid up for me a crown of righteousness, which the Lord, the righteous judge, shall give me at that day: and not to me only, but unto all them also that love his appearing.

–2 Timothy 4:7–8

1971. Good things come to those who *stay awake!*

But know this, that if the goodman of the house had known in what watch the thief would come, he would have watched, and would not have suffered his house to be broken up. Therefore be ye also ready: for in such an hour as ye think not the Son of man cometh.

– Matthew 24:43–44

1972. Anytime a person is doing too much talking, pay close attention not to pay too much attention.

In the multitude of words there wanteth not sin: but he that refraineth his lips is wise.

– Proverbs 10:19

The heart of the righteous studieth to answer: but the mouth of the wicked poureth out evil things.

– Proverbs 15:28

1973. A lot of time, as an avoidance behavior, we make what's not the problem a problem, rather than solving the obvious problem. However, if we would courageously face the real problem, we will get to where we really want to be much faster.

To do justice and judgment is more acceptable to the Lord than sacrifice.

– Proverbs 21:3

1974. No complaints. Just action!

To do justice and judgment is more acceptable to the Lord than sacrifice.

– Proverbs 21:3

1975. The childish complain and remain. The mature respond and go beyond.

When I was a child, I spake as a child, I understood as a child, I thought as a child: but when I became a man, I put away childish things.

–1 Corinthians 13:11

1976. After some time, you mature enough to realize that you are not perfect. The other person is not perfect either. Yet, we each are perfectly ourselves. Neither person is weird. We're just all *fascinatingly different*!

I will praise thee; for I am fearfully and wonderfully made: marvellous are thy works; and that my soul knoweth right well. My substance was not hid from thee, when I was made in secret, and curiously wrought in the lowest parts of the earth. Thine eyes did see my substance, yet being unperfect; and in thy book all my members were written, which in continuance were fashioned, when as yet there was none of them. How precious also are thy thoughts unto me, O God! how great is the sum of them! If I should count them, they are more in number than the sand: when I awake, I am still with thee.

– Psalm 139:14–18

1977. Regarding timing, it's always good to know when to say *when*.

He hath made every thing beautiful in his time: also he hath set the world in their heart, so that no man can find out the work that God maketh from the beginning to the end.

– Ecclesiastes 3:11

1978. People's behavior in your past informs you of their merits to be a part of your *future*.

Whoso keepeth the fig tree shall eat the fruit thereof: so he that waiteth on his master shall be honoured.

– Proverbs 27:18

1979. Regarding destiny, when God gives you an opportunity to escape the land of mediocrity, never look back, because looking back could be deadly to your dreams. Remember *Lot's wife*!

Remember Lot's wife.

– Luke 17:32

1980. The spirit of Satan and the spirit of the world seek to put the righteous under inquisition. However, neither has justification to condemn the righteous.

The wicked watcheth the righteous, and seeketh to slay him. The Lord will not leave him in his hand, nor condemn him when he is judged. Wait on the Lord, and keep his way, and he shall exalt thee to inherit the land: when the wicked are cut off, thou shalt see it. I have seen the wicked in great power, and spreading himself like a green bay tree. Yet he passed away, and, lo, he was not: yea, I sought him, but he could not be found. Mark the perfect man, and behold the upright: for the end of that man is peace.

– Psalm 37:32–37

1981. Regarding equal access in society, you may try to put me out, but you will never *run me off*, due to fear! The earth is the Lord's, and the fullness thereof. We are His people, and the sheep of His pasture.

And in nothing terrified by your adversaries: which is to them an evident token of perdition, but to you of salvation, and that of God.

– Philippians 1:28

1982. We're the "*manifestation generation*." We're not prevented by previous limitations. We have been empowered to change our situations. We are the head and not the tail. We are blessed above all nations. This is a time different than all times in Creation. New chapters are being written into the holy iteration. Your story will be told. Your faith will join the celebration. You're not limited. You are a part of the *manifestation generation!*

For the earnest expectation of the creature waiteth for the manifestation of the sons of God.

– Romans 8:19

1983. I declare God's richest and best blessings upon you now! In Jesus name, amen.

Blessed be the God and Father of our Lord Jesus Christ, who hath blessed us with all spiritual blessings in heavenly places in Christ.

– Ephesians 1:3

1984. No one can stop anyone who takes the time to transform his or her mind. You can't stop an acorn from becoming an oak tree if it's transformed. You can't keep it in the ground. No one can stop anyone who takes the time to transform his or her mind.

I beseech you therefore, brethren, by the mercies of God, that ye present your bodies a living sacrifice, holy, acceptable unto God, which is your reasonable service. And be not conformed to this world: but be ye transformed by the renewing of your mind, that ye may prove what is that good, and acceptable, and perfect, will of God.

– Romans 12:1–2

1985. God's eyes are *"running to and fro"* throughout the earth, looking for someone to bless. Give Him something to bless by obeying His commandment to be fruitful, creative, and productive. His angels are informing Him of those who are at the *peak of ripeness* for a blessing! Let that be you!

For the eyes of the Lord run to and fro throughout the whole earth, to shew himself strong in the behalf of them whose heart is perfect toward him. . .

–2 Chronicles 16:9a

1986. Let excellence be the signature of your work today. Show people who you are by what you do and the attitude you do it in. Represent the high standards of God in all that you do. You are a child of The Most High God.

And over these three presidents; of whom Daniel was first: that the princes might give accounts unto them, and the king should have no damage. Then this Daniel was preferred above the presidents and princes, because an excellent spirit was in him; and the king thought to set him over the whole realm. Then the presidents and princes sought to find occasion against Daniel concerning the kingdom; but they could find none occasion nor fault; forasmuch as he was faithful, neither was there any error or fault found in him.

– Daniel 6:2–4

1987. Our differences in tastes, inclinations, and passions regarding life and career choice are a testament of the Creator's creativity and of His special consideration of us.

Wherefore I perceive that there is nothing better, than that a man should rejoice in his own works; for that is his portion: for who shall bring him to see what shall be after him?

– Ecclesiastes 3:22

1988. Grace and principles release miracles. Both are necessary and reliable for miracles. Miracles are explainable. Grace and principles release miracles.

He that diligently seeketh good procureth favour: but he that seeketh mischief, it shall come unto him.

– Proverbs 11:27

1989. Your Christianity should change your personality. Your Christianity should change your heredity. Your Christianity should change your learned behavior from your original natural locality. You are now born-again. You are born of Heaven. You should act like it!

Therefore if any man be in Christ, he is a new creature: old things are passed away; behold, all things are become new. And all things are of God, who hath reconciled us to himself by Jesus Christ, and hath given to us the ministry of reconciliation; To wit, that God was in Christ, reconciling the world unto himself, not imputing their trespasses unto them; and hath committed unto us the word of reconciliation. Now then we are ambassadors for Christ, as though God did beseech you by us: we pray you in Christ's stead, be ye reconciled to God. For he hath made him to be sin for us, who knew no sin; that we might be made the righteousness of God in him.

—2 Corinthians 5:17–21

1990. Make memories while you *still can remember*!

The memory of the just is blessed: but the name of the wicked shall rot.

– Proverbs 10:7

1991. Slavery has always been a mindset. It has never been a true reality.

Shake thyself from the dust; arise, and sit down, O Jerusalem: loose thyself from the bands of thy neck, O captive daughter of Zion.

– Isaiah 52:2

1992. Regarding opposition, does the elephant feel the kicking of the *ant*? Do not be moved by your adversaries. Just keep on marching forward!

And in nothing terrified by your adversaries: which is to them an evident token of perdition, but to you of salvation, and that of God.

– Philippians 1:28

But none of these things move me, neither count I my life dear unto myself, so that I might finish my course with joy, and the ministry, which I have received of the Lord Jesus, to testify the gospel of the grace of God.

– Acts 20:24

1993. Regarding management, do not be overtaken with anger. Rather, point out the problems, and, then be instructive. Solve by *getting involved*. Dissolve the problems by adding the fresh water of your wisdom and experienced perspective.

To do justice and judgment is more acceptable to the Lord than sacrifice.

– Proverbs 21:3

1994. No matter what life tries to put on you, don't let it take what God gave you!

Peace I leave with you, my peace I give unto you: not as the world giveth, give I unto you. Let not your heart be troubled, neither let it be afraid.

– John 14:27

That the trial of your faith, being much more precious than of gold that perisheth, though it be tried with fire, might be found unto praise and honour and glory at the appearing of Jesus Christ: Whom having not seen, ye love; in whom, though now ye see him not, yet believing, ye rejoice with joy unspeakable and full of glory.

–1 Peter 1:7–8

1995. God allows some things to come to a head, so that you can *pop that zit!*

Moreover the law entered, that the offence might abound. But where sin abounded, grace did much more abound.

– Romans 5:20

1996. Even those who look for perfection are not perfect.

And why beholdest thou the mote that is in thy brother's eye, but considerest not the beam that is in thine own eye? Or how wilt thou say to thy brother, Let me pull out the mote out of thine eye; and, behold, a beam is in thine own eye? Thou hypocrite, first cast out the beam out of thine own eye; and then shalt thou see clearly to cast out the mote out of thy brother's eye.

– Matthew 7:3–5

1997. Regarding giving and receiving, the carnal, fleshly nature seeks to bind you with cords of indebtedness. True love gives wings, not strings. True love is a free gift.

Owe no man any thing, but to love one another: for he that loveth another hath fulfilled the law.

– Romans 13:8

1998. Regarding perspectives on company problems, the difference between employers and employees is like the difference between parents and teenagers. A teenager thinks they know everything concerning how life should go, when they are teenagers. They think their parents know nothing, until they become parents themselves. Then, they realize how much their parents actually knew, and wish they had paid more attention growing up!

A servant will not be corrected by words: for though he understand he will not answer.

– Proverbs 29:19

Whoso keepeth the fig tree shall eat the fruit thereof: so he that waiteth on his master shall be honoured.

– Proverbs 27:18

1999. The week moves fast. The weekend moves even faster. Before you turn around, it's Monday morning. Therefore, you should take heed to how you spend your discretionary time. Choose to live on purpose. Make every moment bring a tangible or intangible benefit. *These are the days of our lives!*

Say not ye, There are yet four months, and then cometh harvest? behold, I say unto you, Lift up your eyes, and look on the fields; for they are white already to harvest.

– John 4:35

2000. It's not good to talk negatively about dead people, out of respect. It's not good to disesteem living people, out of your lack of knowledge of what to expect. As long as anyone is alive, things can turn around for good for that person. So, it's never good to disesteem anyone, because you never know who God can make that person to be in the future!

For to him that is joined to all the living there is hope: for a living dog is better than a dead lion. For the living know that they shall die: but the dead know not any thing, neither have they any more a reward; for the memory of them is forgotten. Also their love, and their hatred, and their envy, is now perished; neither have they any more a portion for ever in any thing that is done under the sun. Go thy way, eat thy bread with joy, and drink thy wine with a merry heart; for God now accepteth thy works. Let thy garments be always white; and let thy head lack no ointment. Live joyfully with the wife whom thou lovest all the days of the life of thy vanity, which he hath given thee under the sun, all the days of thy vanity: for that is thy portion in this life, and in thy labour which thou takest under the sun. Whatsoever thy hand findeth to do, do it with thy might; for there is no work, nor device, nor knowledge, nor wisdom, in the grave, whither thou goest. I returned, and saw under the sun, that the race is not to the swift, nor the battle to the strong, neither yet bread to the wise, nor yet riches to men of understanding, nor yet favour to men of skill; but time and chance happeneth to them all.

– Ecclesiastes 9:4–11

2001. Finance is the discipline of the *purveyors* of the future.

Cast thy bread upon the waters: for thou shalt find it after many days. Give a portion to seven, and also to eight; for thou knowest not what evil shall be upon the earth. If the clouds be full of rain, they empty themselves upon the earth: and if the tree fall toward the south, or toward the north, in the place where the tree falleth, there it shall be. He that observeth the wind shall not sow; and he that regardeth the clouds shall not reap. As thou knowest not what is the way of the spirit, nor how the bones do grow in the womb of her that is with child: even so thou knowest not the works of God who maketh all. In the morning sow thy seed, and in the evening withhold not thine hand: for thou knowest not whether shall prosper, either this or that, or whether they both shall be alike good.

2002. You have to keep doing what you need to do, so you can keep doing what you want to do.

In all labour there is profit: but the talk of the lips tendeth only to penury.

– Proverbs 14:23

For a dream cometh through the multitude of business; and a fools voice is known by multitude of words.

– Ecclesiastes 5:3

2003. When darkness tries to overshadow the land, the light of God's love will always swallow up the darkness! There's a "Light in Goshen" amongst the people of God!

And the Lord said unto Moses, Stretch out thine hand toward heaven, that there may be darkness over the land of Egypt, even darkness which may be felt. And Moses stretched forth his hand toward heaven; and there was a thick darkness in all the land of Egypt three days: They saw not one another, neither rose any from his place for three days: but all the children of Israel had light in their dwellings.

– Exodus 10:21–23

2004. With God on your side, it doesn't matter who comes against you. God will *annihilate* your enemies!

It pleased Darius to set over the kingdom an hundred and twenty princes, which should be over the whole kingdom; And over these three presidents; of whom Daniel was first: that the princes might give accounts unto them, and the king should have no damage. Then this Daniel was preferred above the presidents and princes, because an excellent spirit was in him; and the king thought to set him over the whole realm.

Then the presidents and princes sought to find occasion against Daniel concerning the kingdom; but they could find none occasion nor fault; forasmuch as he was faithful, neither was there any error or fault found in him. Then said these men, We shall not find any occasion against this Daniel, except we find it against him concerning the law of his God. Then these presidents and princes assembled together to the king, and said thus unto him, King Darius, live for ever. All the presidents of the kingdom, the governors, and the princes, the counsellors, and the captains, have consulted together to establish a royal statute, and to make a firm decree, that whosoever shall ask a petition of any God or man for thirty days, save of thee, O king, he shall be cast into the den of lions. Now, O king, establish the decree, and sign the writing, that it be not changed, according to the law of the Medes and Persians, which altereth not. Wherefore king Darius signed the writing and the decree. Now when Daniel knew that the writing was signed, he went into his house; and his windows being open in his chamber toward Jerusalem, he kneeled upon his knees three times a day, and prayed, and gave thanks before his God, as he did aforetime. Then these men assembled, and found Daniel praying and making supplication before his God. Then they came near, and spake before the king concerning the kings decree; Hast thou not signed a decree, that every man that shall ask a petition of any God or man within thirty days, save of thee, O king, shall be cast into the den of lions? The king answered and said, The thing is true, according to the law of the Medes and Persians, which altereth not. Then answered they and said before the king, That Daniel, which is of the children of the captivity of Judah, regardeth not thee, O king, nor the decree that thou hast signed, but maketh his petition three times a day. Then the king, when he heard these words, was sore displeased with himself, and set his heart on Daniel to deliver him: and he laboured till the going down of the sun to deliver him. Then these men assembled unto the king, and said unto the king, Know, O king, that the law of the Medes and Persians is, That no decree nor statute which the king establisheth may be changed. Then the king commanded, and they brought Daniel, and cast him into the den of lions. Now the king spake and said unto Daniel, Thy God whom thou servest continually, he will deliver thee. And a stone was brought, and laid upon the mouth of the den; and the king sealed it with his own signet, and with the signet of his lords; that the purpose might not be changed concerning Daniel. Then the king went to his palace, and passed the night fasting: neither were instruments of musick brought before him: and his sleep went from him. Then the king arose very early in the morning, and went in haste unto the den of lions. And when he came to the den, he cried with a lamentable voice unto Daniel: and the king spake and said to Daniel, O Daniel, servant of the living God, is thy God, whom thou servest continually, able to deliver thee from the lions? Then said Daniel unto the king, O king, live for ever. My God hath sent his angel, and hath shut the lions mouths, that they have not hurt me: forasmuch as before him innocency was found in me; and also before thee, O king, have I done no hurt. Then was the king exceedingly glad for him, and commanded that they should take Daniel up out of the den. So Daniel was taken up out of the den, and no manner of hurt was found upon him, because he believed in his God. And the king commanded, and they brought those men which had accused Daniel, and they cast them into the den of lions, them, their children, and their wives; and the lions had the mastery of them, and brake all their bones in pieces or ever they came at the bottom of the den. Then king Darius wrote unto all people, nations, and languages, that dwell in all the earth; Peace be multiplied unto you. I make a decree, That in every dominion of my kingdom men tremble and fear before the God of Daniel: for he is the living God, and stedfast for ever, and his kingdom that which shall not be destroyed, and his dominion shall be even unto the end. He delivereth and rescueth, and he worketh signs and wonders in heaven and in earth, who hath delivered Daniel from the power of the lions. So this Daniel prospered in the reign of Darius, and in the reign of Cyrus the Persian.

– Daniel 6

2005. The Bible is not politically correct. The Bible is just *correct*. And, if you're wrong, God will correct *you*!

But he that doeth wrong shall receive for the wrong which he hath done: and there is no respect of persons.

– Colossians 3:25

2006. As I read various biographies and autobiographies of certain rich people, I'm left with the conclusion that there is *poor and crazy*, and there is *rich and crazy*. Whether poor or rich, certain people have the tendency to be *crazy*! Only through keeping our minds renewed to the wisdom and ways of God will we all be able to remain sober, stable, and sound minded.

For God hath not given us the spirit of fear; but of power, and of love, and of a sound mind.

−2 Timothy 1:7

2007. Through patience you can enjoy more of life!

In your patience possess ye your souls.

− Luke 21:19

2008. There's one thing about life, people who've never made a mistake, never made an improvement.

In the morning sow thy seed, and in the evening withhold not thine hand: for thou knowest not whether shall prosper, either this or that, or whether they both shall be alike good.

− Ecclesiastes 11:6

2009. Regarding hiring, the skillful, willing, ready, eager worker should get the job. Skillfulness is attainable. The attitude of willing eagerness is a choice of disposition. It speaks of gratitude to do the job. Always hire that person!

Seest thou a man diligent in his business? he shall stand before kings; he shall not stand before mean men.

− Proverbs 22:29

2010. Success can be an event, but wealth is a state of being, from which you can make continual withdrawals.

Thou hast caused men to ride over our heads; we went through fire and through water: but thou broughtest us out into a wealthy place.

– Psalm 66:12

2011. Regarding business, anything that you barely take a step towards getting into and then you find it's hard to get out of, that tells you that you're in *danger*! You've just stepped into *quicksand*! Immediately, determinedly begin to slowly wiggle your way out, and bypass it. Walk all the way to the other side!

A prudent man foreseeth the evil, and hideth himself; but the simple pass on, and are punished.

– Proverbs 27:12

2012. There are no *minor transactions* in life. Everything requires thought and prayer.

The heart of the righteous studieth to answer: but the mouth of the wicked poureth out evil things.

– Proverbs 15:28

2013. It may not always be like clockwork when I respond, but I always respond responsibly.

The heart of the righteous studieth to answer: but the mouth of the wicked poureth out evil things.

— Proverbs 15:28

2014. If you believe that it's worth it, you will make it happen! And, thus, you will make it happen!

This book of the law shall not depart out of thy mouth; but thou shalt meditate therein day and night, that thou mayest observe to do according to all that is written therein: for then thou shalt make thy way prosperous, and then thou shalt have good success.

— Joshua 1:8

2015. Driving in the city is like a bank robbery. If everyone remains calm, nobody gets hurt.

Peace I leave with you, my peace I give unto you: not as the world giveth, give I unto you. Let not your heart be troubled, neither let it be afraid.

— John 14:27

2016. Regarding challenges, believe for the best, prepare for the worst. Either way, God is faithful.

There hath no temptation taken you but such as is common to man: but God is faithful, who will not suffer you to be tempted above that ye are able; but will with the temptation also make a way to escape, that ye may be able to bear it.

–1 Corinthians 10:13

2017. In the midst of storms and floods, we can still choose to say "Thank you Jesus!" Even in devastating weather and situations, we can still choose to praise the Lord, because He's good. God is faithful, and He is able to restore. God knows about every storm or flood that will come against our lives. Yet, He's able to bring us out after the storm into a wealthier place! Blessings are on the way for our nation. This moment is only the storm before the calm. God will give us perfect peace.

Thou wilt keep him in perfect peace, whose mind is stayed on thee: because he trusteth in thee. Trust ye in the Lord for ever: for in the Lord JEHOVAH is everlasting strength:

– Isaiah 26:3–4

2018. The best thing that you can do for your family and for other people is to keep on praying for them. Keep living a righteous life, so that you can get a *prayer through*. Then, keep on praying for them.

Confess your faults one to another, and pray one for another, that ye may be healed. The effectual fervent prayer of a righteous man availeth much. Elias was a man subject to like passions as we are, and he prayed earnestly that it might not rain: and it rained not on the earth by the space of three years and six months. And he prayed again, and the heaven gave rain, and the earth brought forth her fruit.

– James 5:16–18

2019. When life gets down to the *"nitty-gritty"*, don't let the *grits* change you. Rather, you should change the grits. You are *salt* of the earth!

Ye are the salt of the earth: but if the salt have lost his savour, wherewith shall it be salted? it is thenceforth good for nothing, but to be cast out, and to be trodden under foot of men. Ye are the light of the world. A city that is set on an hill cannot be hid. Neither do men light a candle, and put it under a bushel, but on a candlestick; and it giveth light unto all that are in the house. Let your light so shine before men, that they may see your good works, and glorify your Father which is in heaven.

– Matthew 5:13–16

Another parable put he forth unto them, saying, The kingdom of heaven is like to a grain of mustard seed, which a man took, and sowed in his field: which indeed is the least of all seeds: but when it is grown, it is the greatest among herbs, and becometh a tree, so that the birds of the air come and lodge in the branches thereof. Another parable spake he unto them; The kingdom of heaven is like unto leaven, which a woman took, and hid in three measures of meal, till the whole was leavened.

– Matthew 13:31–33

2020. The Word of God is like seeds of light sown into an ocean of darkness. People cling onto that light, like clinging onto a *life raft* during the storms and floods of life.

And Jesus answered him, saying, It is written, That man shall not live by bread alone, but by every word of God.

– Luke 4:4

2021. Being able to see beyond where you are, empowers you to go to where you want to be.

Where there is no vision, the people perish: but he that keepeth the law, happy is he.

– Proverbs 29:18

And the Lord answered me, and said, Write the vision, and make it plain upon tables, that he may run that readeth it. For the vision is yet for an appointed time, but at the end it shall speak, and not lie: though it tarry, wait for it; because it will surely come, it will not tarry. Behold, his soul which is lifted up is not upright in him: but the just shall live by his faith.

– Habakkuk 2:2–4

And they said, Go to, let us build us a city and a tower, whose top may reach unto heaven; and let us make us a name, lest we be scattered abroad upon the face of the whole earth. And the Lord came down to see the city and the tower, which the children of men builded. And the Lord said, Behold, the people is one, and they have all one language; and this they begin to do: and now nothing will be restrained from them, which they have imagined to do.

– Genesis 11:4–6

2022. Regarding excuses, consider the ants, thou sluggard, and always *find a way*!

Go to the ant, thou sluggard; consider her ways, and be wise: which having no guide, overseer, or ruler, provideth her meat in the summer, and gathereth her food in the harvest.

– Proverbs 6:6–8

2023. Regarding business ventures, have the courage of a naive child. Have the caution of an experienced adult. Then, have the willingness to learn what's necessary to make the safest decision. But, do remember, nothing ventured, nothing gained!

For to him that is joined to all the living there is hope: for a living dog is better than a dead lion. For the living know that they shall die: but the dead know not any thing, neither have they any more a reward; for the memory of them is forgotten. Also their love, and their hatred, and their envy, is now perished; neither have they any more a portion for ever in any thing that is done under the sun. Go thy way, eat thy bread with joy, and drink thy wine with a merry heart; for God now accepteth thy works. Let thy garments be always white; and let thy head lack no ointment. Live joyfully with the wife whom thou lovest all the days of the life of thy vanity, which he hath given thee under the sun, all the days of thy vanity: for that is thy portion in this life, and in thy labour which thou takest under the sun. Whatsoever thy hand findeth to do, do it with thy might; for there is no work, nor device, nor knowledge, nor wisdom, in the grave, whither thou goest. I returned, and saw under the sun, that the race is not to the swift, nor the battle to the strong, neither yet bread to the wise, nor yet riches to men of understanding, nor yet favour to men of skill; but time and chance happeneth to them all.

– Ecclesiastes 9:4–11

2024. Some seek to marginalize those who are gifted, talented, or stronger in certain areas than themselves. It's an attempt to bring the gifted down to a level that the average can subdue, control, and manipulate. These "thinkers" seek to rationalize giftedness, and say anyone can learn to be just as good with practice. However, there are some things that are naturally superior in certain individuals. This should be celebrated, rather than marginalized. Yet, we each should be encouraged to maximize our own strengths, through practicing universal principles, such as diligence. Diligence is a virtue that is equally available to all.

It is naught, it is naught, saith the buyer: but when he is gone his way, then he boasteth.

– Proverbs 20:14

Seest thou a man diligent in his business? he shall stand before kings; he shall not stand before mean men.

– Proverbs 22:29

2025. What I don't know, I will learn. What I don't have, I will earn. Make no room for excuses.

Go to the ant, thou sluggard; consider her ways, and be wise: which having no guide, overseer, or ruler, provideth her meat in the summer, and gathereth her food in the harvest.

– Proverbs 6:6–8

2026. Here is a mystery of faith: stretch out farther than you can comfortably see, and God will take you further than where you first may have gone. Your courage to stretch licenses God to take you to the next level He desires to take you to.

Enlarge the place of thy tent, and let them stretch forth the curtains of thine habitations: spare not, lengthen thy cords, and strengthen thy stakes; For thou shalt break forth on the right hand and on the left; and thy seed shall inherit the Gentiles, and make the desolate cities to be inhabited.

– Isaiah 54:2–3

2027. Sometimes God will stretch you beyond your comfort zone, in order to alert you to how far you have already grown.

Enlarge the place of thy tent, and let them stretch forth the curtains of thine habitations: spare not, lengthen thy cords, and strengthen thy stakes; For thou shalt break forth on the right hand and on the left; and thy seed shall inherit the Gentiles, and make the desolate cities to be inhabited.

– Isaiah 54:2–3

2028. Take advantage of every advantage with thanksgiving.

For a great door and effectual is opened unto me, and there are many adversaries.

–1 Corinthians 16:9

2029. We are praying for the people in the path of the hurricane. God is faithful. I declare His protection shields all those in the path of this storm. He does hear the voices of His children. The Word remains true and faithful in spite of any test we may be faced with. God is our refuge and strength, a very present help in time of trouble.

God is our refuge and strength, a very present help in trouble.

– Psalm 46:1

Are not two sparrows sold for a farthing? and one of them shall not fall on the ground without your Father. But the very hairs of your head are all numbered. Fear ye not therefore, ye are of more value than many sparrows.

– Matthew 10:29–31

2030. Find a place of safety during times of storm. Hide yourself from danger. This is practical thinking. Hide your heart in the presence of God during times of trouble. In Him is safety for our souls. Both measures are necessary requirements for remaining alive during the storms of life.

A prudent man foreseeth the evil, and hideth himself; but the simple pass on, and are punished.

– Proverbs 27:12

The name of the Lord is a strong tower: the righteous runneth into it, and is safe.

– Proverbs 18:10

2031. The Bible is not philosophy. The Bible is truth. Obeying it or not obeying it is a matter of life or death.

I call heaven and earth to record this day against you, that I have set before you life and death, blessing and cursing: therefore choose life, that both thou and thy seed may live.

– Deuteronomy 30:19

2032. Other than allergies, you know you're blessed when you can judge whether you will eat food based on the nutritional sticker on the side, rather than simply based on being hungry. Some people would scoff at a Big Mac. Others would think they have died and gone to Heaven to find some beef in addition to that bowl of porridge. It's all a matter of perspective.

The full soul loatheth an honeycomb; but to the hungry soul every bitter thing is sweet.

– Proverbs 27:7

Rejoice evermore. Pray without ceasing. In every thing give thanks: for this is the will of God in Christ Jesus concerning you.

–1 Thessalonians 5:16–18

2033. Don't focus on your problems. Focus on your blessings. If you focus on your blessings, your blessings will multiply.

The blessing of the Lord, it maketh rich, and he addeth no sorrow with it.

– Proverbs 10:22

2034. Learn what you need to learn in order to earn what you want from the Lord. That way, when you receive it, no one can act like they gave you a favor. Rather, you took the time to study and invest what was required in order to obtain what God always wanted you to have. At the end of the day, all you will be required to say is, "Thank You Lord, for fulfilling Your Word unto me!"

And that ye study to be quiet, and to do your own business, and to work with your own hands, as we commanded you; That ye may walk honestly toward them that are without, and that ye may have lack of nothing.

–1 Thessalonians 4:11–12

2035. If God seems to be talking to you about something, yet, you can't quite figure out fully what He's talking about, rest assured in the fact that He fully knows. If you know and trust Him, then, you know enough. You'll understand it better *by and by.*

For I know the thoughts that I think toward you, saith the Lord, thoughts of peace, and not of evil, to give you an expected end.

– Jeremiah 29:11

2036. If you plan on being here, God has a plan for you being here, so start living like you plan on being here.

For I know the thoughts that I think toward you, saith the Lord, thoughts of peace, and not of evil, to give you an expected end.

– Jeremiah 29:11

2037. A good friend will let you know when you need a *mint* in life. In other words, a true friend is not afraid to give you honest feedback on life. Thank God for good friends.

Open rebuke is better than secret love. Faithful are the wounds of a friend; but the kisses of an enemy are deceitful.

– Proverbs 27:5–6

2038. Wealth is a matter of perspective. Elisha, the prophet, didn't give the widow with the "pot of oil" *one thin dime*. He only changed her paradigm from a lack mentality to a wealth mentality. He said, "Go borrow many pots from your neighbors", and she took her one pot and poured into the empty pots, and the oil *multiplied*. It was the key to her wealth. The beginning of wealth is a matter of perspective.

Where there is no vision, the people perish: but he that keepeth the law, happy is he.

– Proverbs 29:18

2039. Everyday is not going to be a *knockout*. What matters most is that you fought the full twelve rounds. You are still the champion, even if you won by a *TKO*

For though we walk in the flesh, we do not war after the flesh: (For the weapons of our warfare are not carnal, but mighty through God to the pulling down of strong holds;) Casting down imaginations, and every high thing that exalteth itself against the knowledge of God, and bringing into captivity every thought to the obedience of Christ.

–2 Corinthians 10:3–5

Finally, my brethren, be strong in the Lord, and in the power of his might. Put on the whole armour of God, that ye may be able to stand against the wiles of the devil. For we wrestle not against flesh and blood, but against principalities, against powers, against the rulers of the darkness of this world, against spiritual wickedness in high places. Wherefore take unto you the whole armour of God, that ye may be able to withstand in the evil day, and having done all, to stand. Stand therefore, having your loins girt about with truth, and having on the breastplate of righteousness; And your feet shod with the preparation of the gospel of peace; Above all, taking the shield of faith, wherewith ye shall be able to quench all the fiery darts of the wicked. And take the helmet of salvation, and the sword of the Spirit, which is the word of God: Praying always with all prayer and supplication in the Spirit, and watching thereunto with all perseverance and supplication for all saints.

– Ephesians 6:10–18

2040. Regarding business, if you know what you're doing, you can compete. And, if you don't know what you're doing, you can learn. Either way, you're a *contender* to compete in business. All you have to do is utilize available knowledge to compete.

Seest thou a man diligent in his business? he shall stand before kings; he shall not stand before mean men.

– Proverbs 22:29

2041. Regarding succeeding, if at first you seem uncertain, continue to take steps, gaining knowledge along the way, and you'll become more and more certain as you go. Learn as you go. Don't let uncertainty stop you. Step out in faith, based on what you do know, and grow as you go. You will increase in certainty as you go, and you will increase in success.

Now faith is the substance of things hoped for, the evidence of things not seen. For by it the elders obtained a good report. Through faith we understand that the worlds were framed by the word of God, so that things which are seen were not made of things which do appear.

– Hebrews 11:1-3

2042. Life is filled with opportunities. Life is filled with choices. The deciding factor is how you choose to take them.

The discretion of a man deferreth his anger; and it is his glory to pass over a transgression.

– Proverbs 19:11

2043. Some things that *stress–out* others, fuels others. There are some things that you're just born for! *Your wealth is in your anointing*!

For we are his workmanship, created in Christ Jesus unto good works, which God hath before ordained that we should walk in them.

– Ephesians 2:10

2044. Life is like *"Shawshank Redemption"*. If you keep chipping at the *wall* of opposition with the sharp instruments of your mind and efforts, you will eventually break through to success!

For a dream cometh through the multitude of business; and a fools voice is known by multitude of words.

– Ecclesiastes 5:3

2045. Always treat people with courtesy, kindness, and consideration. Sometimes people could be hanging on by a thread. *You could be that thread.*

I therefore, the prisoner of the Lord, beseech you that ye walk worthy of the vocation wherewith ye are called, with all lowliness and meekness, with longsuffering, forbearing one another in love; endeavouring to keep the unity of the Spirit in the bond of peace.

– Ephesians 4:1–3

2046. If you get the fire going, by working the spark of genius God has put in you, through practicing, there will come a day when God will throw gasoline on that spark, by giving you an opportunity to flare into a raging success!

For a dream cometh through the multitude of business; and a fools voice is known by multitude of words.

– Ecclesiastes 5:3

2047. If you would truly release the energy of your whole personality, you could power the entire world!

To whom God would make known what is the riches of the glory of this mystery among the Gentiles; which is Christ in you, the hope of glory.

– Colossians 1:27

2048. In regards to investing in opportunities, when faced with the question of should you do it or shouldn't you, it's not a matter of how much money, it's not a matter of how much time; it's a matter of "What do you see?" Always ask the question "What do you see?" The vision will determine the success. If you can detect the size of the vision, you will determine the possibility for success. How clear and how much do you see?

Where there is no vision, the people perish: but he that keepeth the law, happy is he.

– Proverbs 29:18

2049. What do you call a crazy baker? A *doughnut*.

When the chief baker saw that the interpretation was good, he said unto Joseph, I also was in my dream, and, behold, I had three white baskets on my head: And in the uppermost basket there was of all manner of bakemeats for Pharaoh; and the birds did eat them out of the basket upon my head. And Joseph answered and said, This is the interpretation thereof:

The three baskets are three days: Yet within three days shall Pharaoh lift up thy head from off thee, and shall hang thee on a tree; and the birds shall eat thy flesh from off thee. And it came to pass the third day, which was Pharaohs birthday, that he made a feast unto all his servants: and he lifted up the head of the chief butler and of the chief baker among his servants. And he restored the chief butler unto his butlership again; and he gave the cup into Pharaohs hand: But he hanged the chief baker: as Joseph had interpreted to them. Yet did not the chief butler remember Joseph, but forgat him.

– Genesis 40:16–23

Wherefore I put thee in remembrance that thou stir up the gift of God, which is in thee by the putting on of my hands. For God hath not given us the spirit of fear; but of power, and of love, and of a sound mind.

–2 Timothy 1:6–7

2050. Confess wealth and prosperity with your mouth, and believe it in your heart, then take action on what you say, and you will be saved from poverty. If it is true in your heart and actions, it will be true in your life.

Even so faith, if it hath not works, is dead, being alone. Yea, a man may say, Thou hast faith, and I have works: shew me thy faith without thy works, and I will shew thee my faith by my works.

– James 2:17–18

2051. Regarding success, pray fervently, plan carefully, and work diligently. Success is obtainable. It is the will of God for you.

But Jesus answered them, My Father worketh hitherto, and I work.

– John 5:17

2052. Mental liberation leads to emotional liberation. If the Son sets you free from fear, you shall be free indeed.

Then said Jesus to those Jews which believed on him, If ye continue in my word, then are ye my disciples indeed; and ye shall know the truth, and the truth shall make you free.

– John 8:31–32

2053. During times of change is a good time to change. When life is making natural or unusual shifts is a good time to evaluate your life to see where you need to change. It can be during New Years, new months, new weeks, new mornings, new relationships, new administrations, etc. During times of change is a good time to change.

Blessed be the Lord, who daily loadeth us with benefits, even the God of our salvation. Selah.

– Psalm 68:19

2054. It's the small things that make the difference between a winner and loser. Discipline yourself, and lay aside every weight and the sin, which so easily trip you up. You will then be able to cross the finish line as an undeniable *victor*!

Wherefore seeing we also are compassed about with so great a cloud of witnesses, let us lay aside every weight, and the sin which doth so easily beset us, and let us run with patience the race that is set before us, Looking unto Jesus the author and finisher of our faith; who for the joy that was set before him endured the cross, despising the shame, and is set down at the right hand of the throne of God. For consider him that endured such contradiction of sinners against himself, lest ye be wearied and faint in your minds. Ye have not yet resisted unto blood, striving against sin.

– Hebrews 12:1–4

2055. When life takes time to say something to you, it pays to listen. Whether it's the death of a friend or loved one, an unusual symptom or diagnosis, cut–backs in the economy, or a new opportunity for change. When life takes time to say something to you, it pays to listen.

The ear that heareth the reproof of life abideth among the wise.

– Proverbs 15:31

2056. Regarding success and progress, you don't necessarily have to forget where you came from, but you definitely have to *leave*.

Therefore leaving the principles of the doctrine of Christ, let us go on unto perfection; not laying again the foundation of repentance from dead works, and of faith toward God, of the doctrine of baptisms, and of laying on of hands, and of resurrection of the dead, and of eternal judgment. And this will we do, if God permit.

– Hebrews 6:1–3

2057. Regarding relationships, we must intentionally endeavor to keep the unity of the spirit, in the bond of peace. Peace binds people together. Strife separates.

I therefore, the prisoner of the Lord, beseech you that ye walk worthy of the vocation wherewith ye are called, with all lowliness and meekness, with longsuffering, forbearing one another in love; endeavouring to keep the unity of the Spirit in the bond of peace.

– Ephesians 4:1–3

2058. In regard to helping people with problems, you may be able to help them out of a fix, but you can't fix their problem. They still have to do something long-term to fix their own problems.

Brethren, if a man be overtaken in a fault, ye which are spiritual, restore such an one in the spirit of meekness; considering thyself, lest thou also be tempted. Bear ye one another's burdens, and so fulfil the law of Christ. For if a man think himself to be something, when he is nothing, he deceiveth himself. But let every man prove his own work, and then shall he have rejoicing in himself alone, and not in another. For every man shall bear his own burden.

– Galatians 6:1–5

2059. If you're still alive, and your dream is still alive, you can still achieve your dream.

And it came to pass in the morning that his spirit was troubled; and he sent and called for all the magicians of Egypt, and all the wise men thereof: and Pharaoh told them his dream; but there was none that could interpret them unto Pharaoh. Then spake the chief butler unto Pharaoh, saying, I do remember my faults this day: Pharaoh was wroth with his servants, and put me in ward in the captain of the guards house, both me and the chief baker: And we dreamed a dream in one night, I and he; we dreamed each man according to the interpretation of his dream. And there was there with us a young man, an Hebrew, servant to the captain of the guard; and we told him, and he interpreted to us our dreams; to each man according to his dream he did interpret. And it came to pass, as he interpreted to us, so it was; me he restored unto mine office, and him he hanged. Then Pharaoh sent and called Joseph, and they brought him hastily out of the dungeon: and he shaved himself, and changed his raiment, and came in unto

Pharaoh. And Pharaoh said unto Joseph, I have dreamed a dream, and there is none that can interpret it: and I have heard say of thee, that thou canst understand a dream to interpret it. And Joseph answered Pharaoh, saying, It is not in me: God shall give Pharaoh an answer of peace. And Pharaoh said unto Joseph, In my dream, behold, I stood upon the bank of the river: And, behold, there came up out of the river seven kine, fatfleshed and well favoured; and they fed in a meadow: And, behold, seven other kine came up after them, poor and very ill favoured and leanfleshed, such as I never saw in all the land of Egypt for badness: And the lean and the ill favoured kine did eat up the first seven fat kine: And when they had eaten them up, it could not be known that they had eaten them; but they were still ill favoured, as at the beginning. So I awoke. And I saw in my dream, and, behold, seven ears came up in one stalk, full and good: And, behold, seven ears, withered, thin, and blasted with the east wind, sprung up after them: And the thin ears devoured the seven good ears: and I told this unto the magicians; but there was none that could declare it to me. And Joseph said unto Pharaoh, The dream of Pharaoh is one: God hath shewed Pharaoh what he is about to do. The seven good kine are seven years; and the seven good ears are seven years: the dream is one. And the seven thin and ill favoured kine that came up after them are seven years; and the seven empty ears blasted with the east wind shall be seven years of famine. This is the thing which I have spoken unto Pharaoh: What God is about to do he sheweth unto Pharaoh. Behold, there come seven years of great plenty throughout all the land of Egypt: And there shall arise after them seven years of famine; and all the plenty shall be forgotten in the land of Egypt; and the famine shall consume the land; And the plenty shall not be known in the land by reason of that famine following; for it shall be very grievous. And for that the dream was doubled unto Pharaoh twice; it is because the thing is established by God, and God will shortly bring it to pass. Now therefore let Pharaoh look out a man discreet and wise, and set him over the land of Egypt. Let Pharaoh do this, and let him appoint officers over the land, and take up the fifth part of the land of Egypt in the seven plenteous years. And let them gather all the food of those good years that come, and lay up corn under the hand of Pharaoh, and let them keep food in the cities. And that food shall be for store to the land against the seven years of famine, which shall be in the land of Egypt; that the land perish not through the famine. And the thing was good in the eyes of Pharaoh, and in the eyes of all his servants. And Pharaoh said unto his servants, Can we find such a one as this is, a man in whom the Spirit of God is? And Pharaoh said unto Joseph, Forasmuch as God hath shewed thee all this, there is none so discreet and wise as thou art: Thou shalt be over my house, and according unto thy word shall all my people be ruled: only in the throne will I be greater than thou. And Pharaoh said unto Joseph, See, I have set thee over all the land of Egypt. And Pharaoh took off his ring from his hand, and put it upon Joseph's hand, and arrayed him in vestures of fine linen, and put a gold chain about his neck; And he made him to ride in the second chariot which he had; and they cried before him, Bow the knee: and he made him ruler over all the land of Egypt.

– Genesis 41:8–43

2060. Home is where the *wealth* is.

Now there cried a certain woman of the wives of the sons of the prophets unto Elisha, saying, Thy servant my husband is dead; and thou knowest that thy servant did fear the Lord: and the creditor is come to take unto him my two sons to be bondmen. And Elisha said unto her, What shall I do for thee? tell me, what hast thou in the house? And she said, Thine handmaid hath not any thing in the house, save a pot of oil. Then he said, Go, borrow thee vessels abroad of all thy neighbours, even empty vessels; borrow not a few. And when thou art come in, thou shalt shut the door upon thee and upon thy sons, and shalt pour out into all those vessels, and thou shalt set aside that which is full. So she went from him, and shut the door upon her and upon her sons, who brought the vessels to her; and she poured out. And it came to pass, when the vessels were full, that she said unto her son, Bring me yet a vessel. And he said unto her, There is not a vessel more. And the oil stayed. Then she came and told the man of God. And he said, Go, sell the oil, and pay thy debt, and live thou and thy children of the rest.

–2 Kings 4:1–7

Praise ye the Lord. Blessed is the man that feareth the Lord, that delighteth greatly in his commandments. His seed shall be mighty upon earth: the generation of the upright shall be blessed. Wealth and riches shall be in his house: and his righteousness endureth for ever.

– Psalm 112:1–3

2061. Wealth won't *come* without *go!*

Now there cried a certain woman of the wives of the sons of the prophets unto Elisha, saying, Thy servant my husband is dead; and thou knowest that thy servant did fear the Lord: and the creditor is come to take unto him my two sons to be bondmen. And Elisha said unto her, What shall I do for thee? tell me, what hast thou in the house? And she said, Thine handmaid hath not any thing in the house, save a pot of oil. Then he said, Go, borrow thee vessels abroad of all thy neighbours, even empty vessels; borrow not a few. And when thou art come in, thou shalt shut the door upon thee and upon thy sons, and shalt pour out into all those vessels, and thou shalt set aside that which is full. So she went from him, and shut the door upon her and upon her sons, who brought the vessels to her; and she poured out. And it came to pass, when the vessels were full, that she said unto her son, Bring me yet a vessel. And he said unto her, There is not a vessel more. And the oil stayed. Then she came and told the man of God. And he said, Go, sell the oil, and pay thy debt, and live thou and thy children of the rest.

–2 Kings 4:1–7

2062. There are some people who get results through the principles of the Lord Jesus Christ, such as diligence, affirmations, visualization, etc.; yet, they haven't accepted Jesus Christ as *Lord*. He is the Prince of Peace. At the end of the day, even though they got results from the principles, they will not be going to Heaven, because they never knew Him as Lord and Savior, and so He will say, "Depart from me, I never knew you." I encourage you to use His principles, and, most importantly, accept Him as your Lord and Savior.

And I saw a great white throne, and him that sat on it, from whose face the earth and the heaven fled away; and there was found no place for them. And I saw the dead, small and great, stand before God; and the books were opened: and another book was opened, which is the book of life: and the dead were judged out of those things which were written in the books, according to their works. And the sea gave up the dead which were in it; and death and hell delivered up the dead which were in them: and they were judged every man according to their works. And death and hell were cast into the lake of fire. This is the second death. And whosoever was not found written in the book of life was cast into the lake of fire.

– Revelation 20:11–15

2063. A faithful man is not a perfect man. He's just a man faithful to continue striving to be the best that he can be in every situation. He will be faithful to God's principles. He will keep trying. He will keep striving. He will keep standing. He's not perfect. He's just faithful to keep striving to be!

Most men will proclaim every one his own goodness: but a faithful man who can find?

– Proverbs 20:6

Now it came to pass, when the wall was built, and I had set up the doors, and the porters and the singers and the Levites were appointed, That I gave my brother Hanani, and Hananiah the ruler of the palace, charge over Jerusalem: for he was a faithful man, and feared God above many.

– Nehemiah 7:1–2

2064. I thank God for miracles. But even miracles have a cause. We're not called to live by miracles. We are called to live by faith. We are to live in continual abundance. That life is based on eternal, universal principles.

– (From the best selling book,
*Your Wealth Is In Your Anointing: Discover Keys To Releasing
Your Potential* Ch. 8, pg. 113)

The blessing of the Lord, it maketh rich, and he addeth no sorrow with it.

– Proverbs 10:22

2065. Concerning life, look up and onward, and thank God for the past.

Brethren, I count not myself to have apprehended: but this one thing I do, forgetting those things which are behind, and reaching forth unto those things which are before, I press toward the mark for the prize of the high calling of God in Christ Jesus.

– Philippians 3:13–14

2066. Regarding creativity, a lot of times the process can be messy, but when it's finished, it can be *beautiful*!

In the beginning God created the heaven and the earth. And the earth was without form, and void; and darkness was upon the face of the deep. And the Spirit of God moved upon the face of the waters. And God said, Let there be light: and there was light. And God saw the light, that it was good: and God divided the light from the darkness. And God called the light Day, and the darkness he called Night. And the evening and the morning were the first day. And God said, Let there be a firmament in the midst of the waters, and let it divide the waters from the waters. And God made the firmament, and divided the waters which were under the firmament from the waters which were above the firmament: and it was so. And God called the firmament Heaven. And the evening and the morning were the second day. And God said, Let the waters under the heaven be gathered together unto one place, and let the dry land appear: and it was so. And God called the dry land Earth; and the gathering together of the waters called he Seas: and God saw that it was good. And God said, Let the earth bring forth grass, the herb yielding seed, and the fruit tree yielding fruit after his kind, whose seed is in itself, upon the earth: and it was so. And the earth brought forth grass, and herb yielding seed after his kind, and the tree yielding fruit, whose seed was in itself, after his kind: and God saw that it was good. And the evening and the morning were the third day. And God said, Let there be lights in the firmament of the heaven to divide the day from the night; and let them be for signs, and for seasons, and for days, and years: And let them be for lights in the firmament of the heaven to give light upon the earth: and it was so. And God made two great lights; the greater light to rule the day, and the lesser light to rule the night: he made the stars also. And God set them in the firmament of the heaven to give light upon the earth, And to rule over the day and over the night, and to divide the light from the darkness: and God saw that it was good. And the evening and the morning were the fourth day. And God said, Let the waters bring forth abundantly the moving creature that hath life, and fowl that may fly above the earth in the open firmament of heaven. And God created great whales, and every living creature that moveth, which the waters brought forth abundantly, after their kind, and every winged fowl after his kind: and God saw that it was good. And God blessed them, saying, Be fruitful, and multiply, and fill the waters in the seas, and let fowl multiply in the earth. And the evening and the morning were the fifth day. And God said, Let the earth bring forth the living creature after his kind, cattle, and creeping thing, and beast of the earth after his kind: and it was so. And God made the beast of the earth after his kind, and cattle after their kind, and every thing that creepeth upon the earth after his kind: and God saw that it was good. And God said, Let us make man in our image, after our likeness: and let them have dominion over the fish of the sea, and over the fowl of the air, and over the cattle, and over all the earth, and over every creeping thing that creepeth upon the earth. So God created man in his own image, in the image of God created he him; male and female created he them. And God blessed them, and God said unto them, Be fruitful, and multiply, and replenish the earth, and subdue it: and have dominion over the fish of the sea, and over the fowl of the air, and over every living thing that moveth upon the earth. And God said, Behold, I have given you every herb bearing seed, which is upon the face of all the earth, and every tree, in the which is the fruit of a tree yielding seed; to you it shall be for meat. And to every beast of the earth, and to every fowl of the air, and to every thing that creepeth upon the earth, wherein there is life, I have given every green herb for meat: and it was so. And God saw every thing that he had made, and, behold, it was very good. And the evening and the morning were the sixth day.

– Genesis 1

2067. If the saints will focus again on saving souls, a whole lot of our problems will just work themselves out.

Likewise, I say unto you, there is joy in the presence of the angels of God over one sinner that repenteth.

– Luke 15:10

The fruit of the righteous is a tree of life; and he that winneth souls is wise.

– Proverbs 11:30

2068. Regarding problems, don't complain about the *fire* of life. If you are the *real deal*, then, you will shine brighter. Only the *scum* complains about the refiners fire, but the pure gold shines brighter, because it's the *real deal*.

Behold, I have refined thee, but not with silver; I have chosen thee in the furnace of affliction.

– Isaiah 48:10

2069. To be successful spiritually or financially, you have to leave your old crowd. If you want to be saved, you've got to leave your old crowd. If you want to be prosperous, you've got to leave the old crowd. You can't do what you used to do and still have a change for the better.

He that walketh with wise men shall be wise: but a companion of fools shall be destroyed.

– Proverbs 13:20

2070. A lie is never love. Truth is always love. Only truth spoken in love will heal.

But speaking the truth in love, may grow up into him in all things, which is the head, *even* Christ.

– Ephesians 4:15

2071. We should love the United States of America. We should love the opportunity to live in a country that God has blessed, prospered, and protected. We should daily pray for the United States of America, and work in a united way to make it a better nation, and that patriotism and preservation be sustained.

I exhort therefore, that, first of all, supplications, prayers, intercessions, and giving of thanks, be made for all men; For kings, and for all that are in authority; that we may lead a quiet and peaceable life in all godliness and honesty.

−1 Timothy 2:1–2

2072. Take a stand for God's Word, the Bible. That's the only way to bring lasting change.

I exhort therefore, that, first of all, supplications, prayers, intercessions, and giving of thanks, be made for all men; For kings, and for all that are in authority; that we may lead a quiet and peaceable life in all godliness and honesty.

−1 Timothy 2:1–2

2073. There are various ways to stand against inequity and oppression. Rebellion and disrespect is not always the way. Dignity will always stand and speak louder than rebellion and disrespect, because at the end of the day we still have to live together in unity.

Build ye houses, and dwell in them; and plant gardens, and eat the fruit of them; Take ye wives, and beget sons and daughters; and take wives for your sons, and give your daughters to husbands, that they may bear sons and daughters; that ye may be increased there, and not diminished. And seek the peace of the city whither I have caused you to be carried away captives, and pray unto the Lord for it: for in the peace thereof shall ye have peace.

– Jeremiah 29:5–7

2074. Greatness handles things differently than mediocrity.

Build ye houses, and dwell in them; and plant gardens, and eat the fruit of them; Take ye wives, and beget sons and daughters; and take wives for your sons, and give your daughters to husbands, that they may bear sons and daughters; that ye may be increased there, and not diminished. And seek the peace of the city whither I have caused you to be carried away captives, and pray unto the Lord for it: for in the peace thereof shall ye have peace.

– Jeremiah 29:5–7

2075. In life, you've got to do the best that you can, and then *can* the best that you do. Make memories and hold onto them for a lifetime.

For to him that is joined to all the living there is hope: for a living dog is better than a dead lion. For the living know that they shall die: but the dead know not any thing, neither have they any more a reward; for the memory of them is forgotten. Also their love, and their hatred, and their envy, is now perished; neither have they any more a portion for ever in any thing that is done under the sun. Go thy way, eat thy bread with joy, and drink thy wine with a merry heart; for God now accepteth thy works. Let thy garments be always white; and let thy head lack no ointment. Live joyfully with the wife whom thou lovest all the days of the life of thy vanity, which he hath given thee under the sun, all the days of thy vanity: for that is thy portion in this life, and in thy labour which thou takest under the sun. Whatsoever thy hand findeth to do, do it with thy might; for there is no work, nor device, nor knowledge, nor wisdom, in the grave, whither thou goest. I returned, and saw under the sun, that the race is not to the swift, nor the battle to the strong, neither yet bread to the wise, nor yet riches to men of understanding, nor yet favour to men of skill; but time and chance happeneth to them all.

– Ecclesiastes 9:4–11

2076. Just like Oprah Winfrey had the aspiration and ambition to keep striving pass her initial talent and profession as a talk show host, in order to own her *OWN* network, magazine, production studio, etc.; we too should keep striving for ownership of all we have the capacity of acquiring in life. We shouldn't settle for less than we deserve and have a right to.

And that ye study to be quiet, and to do your own business, and to work with your own hands, as we commanded you; that ye may walk honestly toward them that are without, and that ye may have lack of nothing.

−1 Thessalonians 4:11–12

2077. The Gospel is not a *"spell"* that you're under, which leads you to the conclusion that you don't have to do anything to receive the blessings of God. Rather, it is an alerting of the mind to the fact that you are made in the image and likeness of God. It alerts you of the presence of God's Spirit in your human spirit and it encourages you to release Christ in you, the hope of glory. God's expectation is for your success. The true Gospel wakes you up!

The Spirit of the Lord is upon me, because he hath anointed me to preach the gospel to the poor; he hath sent me to heal the brokenhearted, to preach deliverance to the captives, and recovering of sight to the blind, to set at liberty them that are bruised, To preach the acceptable year of the Lord.

– Luke 4:18–19

2078. Regarding humility, you should be as bold as you need to be to do what God called you to do. Make yourself of no reputation, but let your obedience speak for you. At the end of the day, all that can be said of you is "He or (she) obeyed God, and fulfilled God's purpose for their life."

Now it came to pass, when the wall was built, and I had set up the doors, and the porters and the singers and the Levites were appointed, That I gave my brother Hanani, and Hananiah the ruler of the palace, charge over Jerusalem: for he was a faithful man, and feared God above many.

– Nehemiah 7:1–2

2079. In regard to *"kingmakers"*, the king was a king, before you made the king the king. You are a helper along the way. You are a helper of his or her faith, but you do not have dominion over his or her faith. You are a helper of his or her joy.

Not for that we have dominion over your faith, but are helpers of your joy: for by faith ye stand.

−2 Corinthians 1:24

2080. Concerning dreams, a lot of times when you tell someone about your dream, they may say, "Well, we'll see." But, no, it's not "Well, we'll see." Rather, it's, we'll say, then, we will do, and *then*, we will see!

Ask, and it shall be given you; seek, and ye shall find; knock, and it shall be opened unto you: For every one that asketh receiveth; and he that seeketh findeth; and to him that knocketh it shall be opened. Or what man is there of you, whom if his son ask bread, will he give him a stone? Or if he ask a fish, will he give him a serpent? If ye then, being evil, know how to give good gifts unto your children, how much more shall your Father which is in heaven give good things to them that ask him?

– Matthew 7:7–11

2081. Embrace your youth. Make the most of it. Be bold. Be strong. Be courageous. Then, when it's time, thank God for a head full of *white hair*. That's a badge of honor you have grown into.

The glory of young men is their strength: and the beauty of old men is the grey head.

– Proverbs 20:29

2082. There's nothing wrong with "*tooting your own horn*", if you know you are a *golden trumpet*.

That the communication of thy faith may become effectual by the acknowledging of every good thing which is in you in Christ Jesus.

— Philemon 6:1

2083. Many people are trained in *"crookery"* in order to survive in the world's system. However, if we live by honesty we will thrive in God's system. Seek ye first the kingdom of God, and His righteousness, and all these things will be added unto you.

Who is a wise man and endued with knowledge among you? let him shew out of a good conversation his works with meekness of wisdom. But if ye have bitter envying and strife in your hearts, glory not, and lie not against the truth. This wisdom descendeth not from above, but is earthly, sensual, devilish. For where envying and strife is, there is confusion and every evil work. But the wisdom that is from above is first pure, then peaceable, gentle, and easy to be intreated, full of mercy and good fruits, without partiality, and without hypocrisy. And the fruit of righteousness is sown in peace of them that make peace.

— James 3:13–18

2084. Conversations are just like driving through a drive–through. Always assume that at least 50% of the important requested content might have been left out! Always check your *bag* before simply driving off with what you're handed.

The simple believeth every word: but the prudent man looketh well to his going.

– Proverbs 14:15

2085. If you'll spend the time that you spend talking about the problem, praying about the problem, you'll solve the problem.

If any of you lack wisdom, let him ask of God, that giveth to all men liberally, and upbraideth not; and it shall be given him.

– James 1:5

2086. In regard to happiness, focus on what God has already done, and put your faith in what He's capable of doing, and you'll be less stressed and you'll be happier. You'll live by faith, full of joy and expectancy! And you'll have hope for your future. Your chief aim should be your future.

Where there is no vision, the people perish: but he that keepeth the law, happy is he.

– Proverbs 29:18

2087. Problem prevention is the key to solving problems.

The beginning of strife is as when one letteth out water: therefore leave off contention, before it be meddled with.

– Proverbs 17:14

2088. Let us continue to pray for the current needs in our society. Pray for those recovering from the storms and flooding. Pray for earthquake victims. And, certainly pray for the families of those that have been victims of violence in our nation. God will hear the prayers of His people for things large and small. Just keep on praying. Stay connected to Heaven.

If my people, which are called by my name, shall humble themselves, and pray, and seek my face, and turn from their wicked ways; then will I hear from heaven, and will forgive their sin, and will heal their land.

–2 Chronicles 7:14

I exhort therefore, that, first of all, supplications, prayers, intercessions, and giving of thanks, be made for all men; For kings, and for all that are in authority; that we may lead a quiet and peaceable life in all godliness and honesty.

–1 Timothy 2:1–2

2089. You can never be free based on a lie. You can be self-deceived based on a lie. You can even be *"happy"* based on a lie. But, you can never be truly free based on a lie.

Then said Jesus to those Jews which believed on him, If ye continue in my word, then are ye my disciples indeed; and ye shall know the truth, and the truth shall make you free.

– John 8:31–32

Open rebuke is better than secret love. Faithful are the wounds of a friend; but the kisses of an enemy are deceitful.

– Proverbs 27:5–6

2090. Concerning faith, you don't need a *co–signer* regarding your faith. You must hear from God for yourself. You must get your assignment. You must know your own heart. You must be sure you are lined up with the Bible. Then, you must know you're right, and go ahead on! You don't need a co–signer on your faith.

And the Lord answered me, and said, Write the vision, and make it plain upon tables, that he may run that readeth it. For the vision is yet for an appointed time, but at the end it shall speak, and not lie: though it tarry, wait for it; because it will surely come, it will not tarry. Behold, his soul which is lifted up is not upright in him: but the just shall live by his faith.

– Habakkuk 2:2–4

But when it pleased God, who separated me from my mothers womb, and called me by his grace, to reveal his Son in me, that I might preach him among the heathen; immediately I conferred not with flesh and blood: neither went I up to Jerusalem to them which were apostles before me; but I went into Arabia, and returned again unto Damascus. Then after three years I went up to Jerusalem to see Peter, and abode with him fifteen days. But other of the apostles saw I none, save James the Lord's brother.

– Galatians 1:15–19

2091. Life is good when you have the *favor factor*! You know that no matter what comes, you're always on the *winning* side.

For thou, Lord, wilt bless the righteous; with favour wilt thou compass him as with a shield.

— Psalm 5:12

2092. Consistency is the key to stability. Stay in the Word day and night. Rejoice in the Lord always, and again, I say, rejoice! Pray without ceasing. Work out your own salvation, with fear and trembling. In other words, be diligent in your pursuit of maintaining a close, intimate relationship with the Lord Jesus Christ. Your relationship with Him is the source of wealth and fullness of life! Consistency is the key to stability.

This book of the law shall not depart out of thy mouth; but thou shalt meditate therein day and night, that thou mayest observe to do according to all that is written therein: for then thou shalt make thy way prosperous, and then thou shalt have good success.

— Joshua 1:8

2093. When you *spendeth* money goeth. When you *soweth* money cometh. But, you still have to be wise in your money management.

Be thou diligent to know the state of thy flocks, and look well to thy herds. For riches are not for ever: and doth the crown endure to every generation? The hay appeareth, and the tender grass sheweth itself, and herbs of the mountains are gathered. The lambs are for thy clothing, and the goats are the price of the field. And thou shalt have goats milk enough for thy food, for the food of thy household, and for the maintenance for thy maidens.

– Proverbs 27:23–27

2094. Regarding influence, either you will be shaped or you will be a *shaper*. In most cases, it will be both. There is no neutral ground.

I beseech you therefore, brethren, by the mercies of God, that ye present your bodies a living sacrifice, holy, acceptable unto God, which is your reasonable service. And be not conformed to this world: but be ye transformed by the renewing of your mind, that ye may prove what is that good, and acceptable, and perfect, will of God.

– Romans 12:1–2

2095. "Your gift looks good on you, and you wear it well."

–Donald Lawrence
(Legendary, Gospel Music Artist)

For thou, Lord, wilt bless the righteous; with favour wilt thou compass him as with a shield.

– Psalm 5:12

2096. Regarding budgeting, savings, investing, exercising, family time, church attendance, etc., the key to lasting success is a regular schedule, not a random schedule.

Be thou diligent to know the state of thy flocks, and look well to thy herds. For riches are not for ever: and doth the crown endure to every generation? The hay appeareth, and the tender grass sheweth itself, and herbs of the mountains are gathered. The lambs are for thy clothing, and the goats are the price of the field. And thou shalt have goats milk enough for thy food, for the food of thy household, and for the maintenance for thy maidens.

– Proverbs 27:23–27

2097. Regarding other people's business, assumption usually reveals ignorance. Tend to your own business, because that's the only place that you are most qualified to be an expert.

And that ye study to be quiet, and to do your own business, and to work with your own hands, as we commanded you; that ye may walk honestly toward them that are without, and that ye may have lack of nothing.

–1 Thessalonians 4:11–12

2098. The instructions of God bring structure to our lives. If we build our lives upon the instructions of the Bible, our lives will be more stable.

Whoso loveth instruction loveth knowledge: but he that hateth reproof is brutish.

– Proverbs 12:1

Therefore, whosoever heareth these sayings of mine, and doeth them, I will liken him unto a wise man, which built his house upon a rock: And the rain descended, and the floods came, and the winds blew, and beat upon that house; and it fell not: for it was founded upon a rock. And every one that heareth these sayings of mine, and doeth them not, shall be likened unto a foolish man, which built his house upon the sand: And the rain descended, and the floods came, and the winds blew, and beat upon that house; and it fell: and great was the fall of it.

– Matthew 7:24–27

2099. Regarding success and progress, the words "I agree" are two of the most powerful words in regard to cooperation with others and with God. "I agree."

Can two walk together, except they be agreed?

– Amos 3:3

Again, I say unto you, That if two of you shall agree on earth as touching any thing that they shall ask, it shall be done for them of my Father which is in heaven.

– Matthew 18:19

2100. The Word of God will *blow your natural mind*! It will get you saved. It will get you healed. It will get you delivered. So, be careful with the Word, because it will transform your life by blowing your *natural mind*!

I beseech you therefore, brethren, by the mercies of God, that ye present your bodies a living sacrifice, holy, acceptable unto God, which is your reasonable service. And be not conformed to this world: but be ye transformed by the renewing of your mind, that ye may prove what is that good, and acceptable, and perfect, will of God.

– Romans 12:1–2

2101. Just because you don't hear my prayers, doesn't mean God doesn't. The effectual, fervent prayers of a righteous person avails much.

And when thou prayest, thou shalt not be as the hypocrites are: for they love to pray standing in the synagogues and in the corners of the streets, that they may be seen of men. Verily I say unto you, They have their reward. But thou, when thou prayest, enter into thy closet, and when thou hast shut thy door, pray to thy Father which is in secret; and thy Father which seeth in secret shall reward thee openly.

– Matthew 6:5–6

2102. One thing about God is that He doesn't count people out for lack of perfection. But, He does measure intent.

For the word of God is quick, and powerful, and sharper than any twoedged sword, piercing even to the dividing asunder of soul and spirit, and of the joints and marrow, and is a discerner of the thoughts and intents of the heart. Neither is there any creature that is not manifest in his sight: but all things are naked and opened unto the eyes of him with whom we have to do. Seeing then that we have a great high priest, that is passed into the heavens, Jesus the Son of God, let us hold fast our profession. For we have not an high priest which cannot be touched with the feeling of our infirmities; but was in all points tempted like as we are, yet without sin. Let us therefore come boldly unto the throne of grace, that we may obtain mercy, and find grace to help in time of need.

– Hebrews 4:12–16

2103. May God's hand of mercy sweep across America and the other nations of the world. I pray that He will heal the hurting and devastated. I pray that He will encourage the brokenhearted. I pray that He will mend the wounded. I pray that He will restore hope to the hopeless. In Jesus name, amen.

The Lord is gracious, and full of compassion; slow to anger, and of great mercy.

– Psalm 145:8

If my people, which are called by my name, shall humble themselves, and pray, and seek my face, and turn from their wicked ways; then will I hear from heaven, and will forgive their sin, and will heal their land.

–2 Chronicles 7:14

2104. "Purpose is the *why*. Focus helps you see the *how*. Passion *fuels* the vision."

– (From the bestselling book *Your Wealth Is In Your Anointing: Discover Keys To Releasing Your Potential*.)

2105. The Words of God are like living stones cast upon the sea of life. No matter how stormy your life may become, if you keep stepping out on the Words of Jesus, you will make it safely to the other side.

And straightway Jesus constrained his disciples to get into a ship, and to go before him unto the other side, while he sent the multitudes away. And when he had sent the multitudes away, he went up into a mountain apart to pray: and when the evening was come, he was there alone. But the ship was now in the midst of the sea, tossed with waves: for the wind was contrary. And in the fourth watch of the night Jesus went unto them, walking on the sea. And when the disciples saw him walking on the sea, they were troubled, saying, It is a spirit; and they cried out for fear. But straightway Jesus spake unto them, saying, Be of good cheer; it is I; be not afraid. And Peter answered him and said, Lord, if it be thou, bid me come unto thee on the water. And he said, Come. And when Peter was come down out of the ship, he walked on the water, to go to Jesus. But when he saw the wind boisterous, he was afraid; and beginning to sink, he cried, saying, Lord, save me. And immediately Jesus stretched forth his hand, and caught him, and said unto him, O thou of little faith, wherefore didst thou doubt? And when they were come into the ship, the wind ceased. Then they that were in the ship came and worshipped him, saying, Of a truth thou art the Son of God.

– Matthew 14:22–33

2106. The best investment that you can make into your future is *motivation*!

Where there is no vision, the people perish: but he that keepeth the law, happy is he.

– Proverbs 29:18

2107. He is a friend who forces you to hunt for your own food, catch your own fish, and harvest your own field. He is a foe who feeds you with welfare without labor.

Blessed is every one that feareth the Lord; that walketh in his ways. For thou shalt eat the labour of thine hands: happy shalt thou be, and it shall be well with thee. Thy wife shall be as a fruitful vine by the sides of thine house: thy children like olive plants round about thy table. Behold, that thus shall the man be blessed that feareth the Lord. The Lord shall bless thee out of Zion: and thou shalt see the good of Jerusalem all the days of thy life. Yea, thou shalt see thy childrens children, and peace upon Israel.

– Psalm 128

2108. There's more to the story, than what's been told. There's more to the *Book*, then what's been sold.

But thou, O Daniel, shut up the words, and seal the book, even to the time of the end: many shall run to and fro, and knowledge shall be increased.

– Daniel 12:4

2109. Husbands and wives wear his and her *"seventy times seven"* card on their left ring finger. That's the true *"get out of jail free card"*. Or, off the sofa!

Then came Peter to him, and said, Lord, how oft shall my brother sin against me, and I forgive him? till seven times? Jesus saith unto him, I say not unto thee, Until seven times: but, Until seventy times seven.

– Matthew 18:21–22

2110. Regarding salvation by faith, I would rather still have questions about all the facts on my deathbed, yet have the blessed assurance of eternal life, than to think I have discovered a new truth, and lose my soul for eternity.

Jesus saith unto him, I am the way, the truth, and the life: no man cometh unto the Father, but by me.

– John 14:6

For as I passed by, and beheld your devotions, I found an altar with this inscription, To The Unknown God. Whom therefore ye ignorantly worship, him declare I unto you. God that made the world and all things therein, seeing that he is Lord of heaven and earth, dwelleth not in temples made with hands; Neither is worshipped with men's hands, as though he needed any thing, seeing he giveth to all life, and breath, and all things; And hath made of one blood all nations of men for to dwell on all the face of the earth, and hath determined the times before appointed, and the bounds of their habitation; That they should seek the Lord, if haply they might feel after him, and find him, though he be not far from every one of us: For in him we live, and move, and have our being; as certain also of your own poets have said, For we are also his offspring.

– Acts 17:23–28

Be it known unto you all, and to all the people of Israel, that by the name of Jesus Christ of Nazareth, whom ye crucified, whom God raised from the dead, *even* by him doth this man stand here before you whole. This is the stone which was set at nought of you builders, which is become the head of the corner. Neither is there salvation in any other: for there is none other name under heaven given among men, whereby we must be saved.

– Acts 4:10–12

2111. People who practice high values have greater practical value. People who practice low or no values have lesser practical value. The practice of values will determine if you're "good for *something*" or "good for *nothing*" or not as useful as you could be. We can always choose to increase our adherence to godly values, and thereby increase in practical value.

But in a great house there are not only vessels of gold and of silver, but also of wood and of earth; and some to honour, and some to dishonour. If a man therefore purge himself from these, he shall be a vessel unto honour, sanctified, and meet for the master's use, and prepared unto every good work. Flee also youthful lusts: but follow righteousness, faith, charity, peace, with them that call on the Lord out of a pure heart.

–2 Timothy 2:20–22

2112. Regarding success, it takes a lot to start it up. It takes a lot to build it up. And, if you want to keep it up, it takes a lot to *keep it up*!

For a dream cometh through the multitude of business; and a fools voice is known by multitude of words.

– Ecclesiastes 5:3

2113. Proven knowledge is always wrong to the person who knows it all.

If a wise man contendeth with a foolish man, whether he rage or laugh, there is no rest.

– Proverbs 29:9

Answer not a fool according to his folly, lest thou also be like unto him. Answer a fool according to his folly, lest he be wise in his own conceit.

– Proverbs 26:4–5

2114. Two words are keys to promotion for men and women to learn as early as possible: circumspection and discretion. If you don't know what either of these mean, that's probably a good sign you should look them up in the dictionary. They are critical to your successful future.

The proverbs of Solomon the son of David, king of Israel; To know wisdom and instruction; to perceive the words of understanding; To receive the instruction of wisdom, justice, and judgment, and equity; To give subtilty to the simple, to the young man knowledge and discretion.

– Proverbs 1:1–4

As a jewel of gold in a swine's snout, so is a fair woman which is without discretion.

– Proverbs 11:22

2115. When you find someone who gives outstanding service, you can simply say to him or her "I don't know where you're coming from, but I know where you're going. You're going straight to the top!" Because, a positive attitude will take you straight to the top!

Seest thou a man diligent in his business? he shall stand before kings; he shall not stand before mean men.

– Proverbs 22:29

2116. Leadership or management can be of two different forms. Either, it can be punitive, corrective, and condemning, or it can be inspiring, uplifting, and affirming. The one will get one form of results, and the other will get another. Inspiring leadership builds people up and causes them to grow, increase, and be their very best.

He chose David also his servant, and took him from the sheepfolds: From following the ewes great with young he brought him to feed Jacob his people, and Israel his inheritance. So he fed them according to the integrity of his heart; and guided them by the skilfulness of his hands.

– Psalm 78:70–72

2117. If you're getting paid big money for being in management, don't complain about big problems. You're not being paid the big money to handle the routine parts of your job. Rather, you're being paid to solve the problems. That's where you make your money. Minimum wage is the pay for minimum problems. Maximum wages require maximum *wisdom*.

And the Lord said, Who then is that faithful and wise steward, whom his lord shall make ruler over his household, to give them their portion of meat in due season? Blessed is that servant, whom his lord when he cometh shall find so doing. Of a truth I say unto you, that he will make him ruler over all that he hath. But and if that servant say in his heart, My lord delayeth his coming; and shall begin to beat the menservants and maidens, and to eat and drink, and to be drunken; The lord of that servant will come in a day when he looketh not for him, and at an hour when he is not aware, and will cut him in sunder, and will appoint him his portion with the unbelievers. And that servant, which knew his lords will, and prepared not himself, neither did according to his will, shall be beaten with many stripes. But he that knew not, and did commit things worthy of stripes, shall be beaten with few stripes. For unto whomsoever much is given, of him shall be much required: and to whom men have committed much, of him they will ask the more.

– Luke 12:42–48

2118. Skill, education, and determination can change your situation and station in life. Get it, and use it!

Seest thou a man diligent in his business? he shall stand before kings; he shall not stand before mean men.

– Proverbs 22:29

Wisdom is the principal thing; therefore get wisdom: and with all thy getting get understanding.

– Proverbs 4:7

A man's gift maketh room for him, and bringeth him before great men.

> – Proverbs 18:16

2119. Regarding trouble, it's better to ignore insignificant trouble that doesn't belong to you.

And in nothing terrified by your adversaries: which is to them an evident token of perdition, but to you of salvation, and that of God.

> – Philippians 1:28

2120. The same God who's real in my worship is the same God who's real in my warfare!

For though we walk in the flesh, we do not war after the flesh: (For the weapons of our warfare are not carnal, but mighty through God to the pulling down of strong holds;) Casting down imaginations, and every high thing that exalteth itself against the knowledge of God, and bringing into captivity every thought to the obedience of Christ.

> –2 Corinthians 10:3–5

And it came to pass that night, that the angel of the Lord went out, and smote in the camp of the Assyrians an hundred fourscore and five thousand: and when they arose early in the morning, behold, they were all dead corpses.

> –2 Kings 19:35

2121. Regarding insincerity, porridge can be tasty and full of nutrition, but just a little bit of strychnine added can still kill you!

The simple believeth every word: but the prudent man looketh well to his going.

– Proverbs 14:15

2122. The dignity of the flesh is characterized by pride, conceit, envy, malice, revenge, and competition. The dignity of the born–again spirit is characterized by the fruit of the spirit, which is love, joy, peace, long–suffering, gentleness, goodness, faith, meekness, and temperance. The flesh is like the characteristics of the prince of the power of the air, Satan. The born–again spirit is like the characteristics of the King of Kings, Jesus Christ. We each can choose the form of dignity we want to portray.

Now the works of the flesh are manifest, which are these; Adultery, fornication, uncleanness, lasciviousness, Idolatry, witchcraft, hatred, variance, emulations, wrath, strife, seditions, heresies, Envyings, murders, drunkenness, revellings, and such like: of the which I tell you before, as I have also told you in time past, that they which do such things shall not inherit the kingdom of God. But the fruit of the Spirit is love, joy, peace, longsuffering, gentleness, goodness, faith, Meekness, temperance: against such there is no law. And they that are Christs have crucified the flesh with the affections and lusts. If we live in the Spirit, let us also walk in the Spirit.

– Galatians 5:19–25

2123. Life is a given. What you make of it is up to you!

For to him that is joined to all the living there is hope: for a living dog is better than a dead lion. For the living know that they shall die: but the dead know not any thing, neither have they any more a reward; for the memory of them is forgotten. Also their love, and their hatred, and their envy, is now perished; neither have they any more a portion for ever in any thing that is done under the sun. Go thy way, eat thy bread with joy, and drink thy wine with a merry heart; for God now accepteth thy works. Let thy garments be always white; and let thy head lack no ointment. Live joyfully with the wife whom thou lovest all the days of the life of thy vanity, which he hath given thee under the sun, all the days of thy vanity: for that is thy portion in this life, and in thy labour which thou takest under the sun. Whatsoever thy hand findeth to do, do it with thy might; for there is no work, nor device, nor knowledge, nor wisdom, in the grave, whither thou goest. I returned, and saw under the sun, that the race is not to the swift, nor the battle to the strong, neither yet bread to the wise, nor yet riches to men of understanding, nor yet favour to men of skill; but time and chance happeneth to them all.

– Ecclesiastes 9:4–11

2124. Success takes time, but if you take the time, you will succeed.

In all labour there is profit: but the talk of the lips tendeth only to penury.

— Proverbs 14:23

For a dream cometh through the multitude of business; and a fools voice is known by multitude of words.

— Ecclesiastes 5:3

2125. Refine your gifts and talents. Turn them into skills. Get your education. Put forth effort, and you will guarantee a profitable result.

Seest thou a man diligent in his business? he shall stand before kings; he shall not stand before mean men.

— Proverbs 22:29

2126. Success is easier said than done, but when it is said, it is granted permission to be done.

Thou shalt also decree a thing, and it shall be established unto thee: and the light shall shine upon thy ways.

— Job 22:28

2127. Regarding life and work, giving yourself a break, will keep you from breaking.

It is vain for you to rise up early, to sit up late, to eat the bread of sorrows: for so he giveth his beloved sleep.

– Psalms 126:2

And he said unto them, Come ye yourselves apart into a desert place, and rest a while: for there were many coming and going, and they had no leisure so much as to eat.

– Mark 6:31

Thus the heavens and the earth were finished, and all the host of them. And on the seventh day God ended his work which he had made; and he rested on the seventh day from all his work which he had made.

– Genesis 2:1–2

2128. Regarding breakfast, a good start will keep you going strong.

And as he lay and slept under a juniper tree, behold, then an angel touched him, and said unto him, Arise and eat. And he looked, and, behold, there was a cake baken on the coals, and a cruse of water at his head. And he did eat and drink, and laid him down again. And the angel of the Lord came again the second time, and touched him, and said, Arise and eat; because the journey is too great for thee. And he arose, and did eat and drink, and went in the strength of that meat forty days and forty nights unto Horeb the mount of God.

–1 Kings 19:5–8

2129. Without ambition there's no *ignition*. Faith is the substance of things *hoped for*!

Now faith is the substance of things hoped for, the evidence of things not seen. For by it the elders obtained a good report.

– Hebrews 11:1–2

2130. Words are valuable. So, make your words count for something that will last for eternity.

Either make the tree good, and his fruit good; or else make the tree corrupt, and his fruit corrupt: for the tree is known by his fruit. O generation of vipers, how can ye, being evil, speak good things? for out of the abundance of the heart the mouth speaketh. A good man out of the good treasure of the heart bringeth forth good things: and an evil man out of the evil treasure bringeth forth evil things. But I say unto you, That every idle word that men shall speak, they shall give account thereof in the day of judgment. For by thy words thou shalt be justified, and by thy words thou shalt be condemned.

– Matthew 12:33–37

2131. In your patience, you maintain possession of your own soul. You will not be flailed about in life by circumstances, people's personalities, places, or events. You will maintain the rudder of your own ship on the, sometimes unpredictable, ocean of life.

He that is slow to anger is better than the mighty; and he that ruleth his spirit than he that taketh a city.

– Proverbs 16:32

In your patience possess ye your souls.

– Luke 21:19

And Jesus stood before the governor: and the governor asked him, saying, Art thou the King of the Jews? And Jesus said unto him, Thou sayest. And when he was accused of the chief priests and elders, he answered nothing. Then said Pilate unto him, Hearest thou not how many things they witness against thee? And he answered him to never a word; insomuch that the governor marvelled greatly.

– Matthew 27:11–14

Final Word

Now that you have enjoyed ***Distinguished Wisdom Presents...
Living Proverbs–Vol. 4***, I encourage you to read this book
daily. Use it as a reference book for continual counsel. Many
readers of the ***"Living Proverbs"*** series have indicated the
words helped to deliver their mind. One reader even gave the
book to a person addicted to drugs, and they were able to find
wisdom for a better way of thinking. If the mind can get free,
the life can get free. The words brought peace and
deliverance. God's Word is a healer. As you renew your mind
to His Word you will be set free. Proverbs 4:7 says, "Wisdom
is the principal thing; therefore get wisdom: and with all thy
getting get understanding." Therefore, I recommend that you
take time to read this book over again, and allow these truths
to free you. Jesus said these words in John 8:31–32 and 36:

> Then said Jesus to those Jews, which believed
> on him, If ye continue in my word, then are ye
> my disciples indeed: And ye shall know the
> truth, and the truth shall make you free. If the

son therefore shall make you free, you shall be
free indeed.

God's Word is what makes us free. As we renew our mind to
God's Word our lives will be changed. We will enjoy the best
that He desires for us. We will be able to teach our children,
grandchildren, and those that we come in contact with how to
be free indeed. Therefore, as you read this book **Distinguished
Wisdom Presents... Living Proverbs—Vol.4**, my prayer is *"May
your life be enriched by the words of wisdom!"* Be sure to look
for the audiobook at
www.TerranceTurnerLivingProverbs.com. Also, you can find
other of my books at www.TerranceTurnerBooks.com. My
books, as well as my gospel music projects are also available
on Amazon.com. Please look for these resources. You will be
further enriched as you hear the words of the author in an
audiobook, as well as experience anointed worship music
from my wife and I, "Terrance & Avis Turner".

About The Author

Pastor Terrance Levise Turner is the senior pastor of Faith Country Holiness Church, in Gallatin, TN. Pastor Turner has an MBA in Finance and Supply Chain Management from Tennessee State University. He also has a bachelors degree in Speech Communications and Theater, with a concentration in mass media from Tennessee State University. He is the president of Well Spoken Inc., a communications company, in Nashville, TN., which focuses on audiobooks, book publishing, and professional speaking. Pastor Turner is the author of several books, including the ***"Living Proverbs"*** series, ***Your Wealth Is In Your Anointing: Discover Keys To Releasing Your Potential***, and ***The Dynamic Victory Confession: Powerful Confessions For A Victorious Life***. For more information visit www.TerranceTurnerBooks.com or www.TerranceTurnerLivingProverbs.com. Or email WellSpokenInc@bellsouth.net. Pastor Turner is also a songwriter and recording artist, with his wife, Avis. His music is available on Amazon.com, ITunes, or at his website www.FaithCountryProductions.com. He continues to serve the community and Body of Christ through service, music, preaching and teaching the Word of God. He and his wife, Avis live in Nashville, TN.